Bare Landscapes

Schiffer Publishing Ltd

4880 Lower Valley Road Atglen, Pennsylvania 19310

Library of Congress Control Number: 2011920406

Type set in Century Gothic/Century Gothic

ISBN: 978-0-7643-3797-0
Printed in Hong Kong

Published by Schiffer Publishing Ltd.
4880 Lower Valley Road
Atglen, PA 19310
Phone: (610) 593-1777; Fax: (610) 593-2002
E-mail: Info@schifferbooks.com

In Europe, Schiffer books are distributed by
Bushwood Books
6 Marksbury Ave.
Kew Gardens
Surrey TW9 4JF England
Phone: 44 (0) 20 8392 8585; Fax: 44 (0) 20 8392 9876
E-mail: info@bushwoodbooks.co.uk
Website: www.bushwoodbooks.co.uk

Bare Landscapes

Sigthor Markusson

Thanks to the models:

Hulda Lind Kristinsdóttir
Heiðrún Arna
Perla Benediktsdóttir
Andrea Diljá Ólafsdóttir
Rosa Lilly
Helga Lilja
Halla Halldórsdóttir
Lára Magnúsdóttir
Guðrún H. Reynisdóttir
Iris MB
Kristín Ósk
Helena Dröfn
Sif Gunnarsdóttir
Sólrún A.S.
Perla Vilhjálmsdóttir
Elísabet Atladóttir

Special thanks to:

Mogens Løwe Markússon
Dagbjört Þorsteinsdóttir
Júlíana Bryndís Sigþórsdóttir
Jamie Lee Hadley
Hafsteinn Viktorsson
Högni Hróarsson
Mary Andersen
Kristján Maack
Rupert Nadeau

Bare Landscapes

Photography by Sigthor Markusson

Poetry by Anna S. Björnsdóttir

Foreword

Bare Landscapes unfolds on an island of extremes, moored far from the madding crowd, in a land of light and darkness. There the seasons are split between the midnight sun of summer and the long brooding hours of winter's dark, cold breath. Under these shades of sun and moon the earth is active and breathing in pools of bubbling water, live volcanoes, and turbulent earthquakes. From that physical cauldron the ground has been torn, twisted, and reshaped into formations as unique as the lines etched into an old face.

In a photograph, it is the light that illuminates the subject, but it's the shadows that hold the secrets. In the best sense of that alliance, the beauty that stays with us often thrives on the displacement of our expectations. We recognize the pieces, but the whole unfolds before us in a new way. We see everything fresh, because it was created that way. The photographs in Bare Landscapes are a beautiful manifestation of this magic of balance and discovery.

Sigthor Markusson is not a magician by trade, but make no mistake there is alchemy at work in these elemental images of flesh and stone. In this photographic journey across the topography of Iceland, the ride is mesmerizing because it is an exploration of two bodies, that of the land and the female form. They are both exposed as they were born, raw and primal, naked and austere, unadorned and blooming. Whether resolved against volcanic rock, sequestered in craters of ice or simmering in hot springs, these stark primordial landscapes are chiseled out of time, untouched in their natural beauty, like the feminine forms that grace them.

Rupert Nadeau

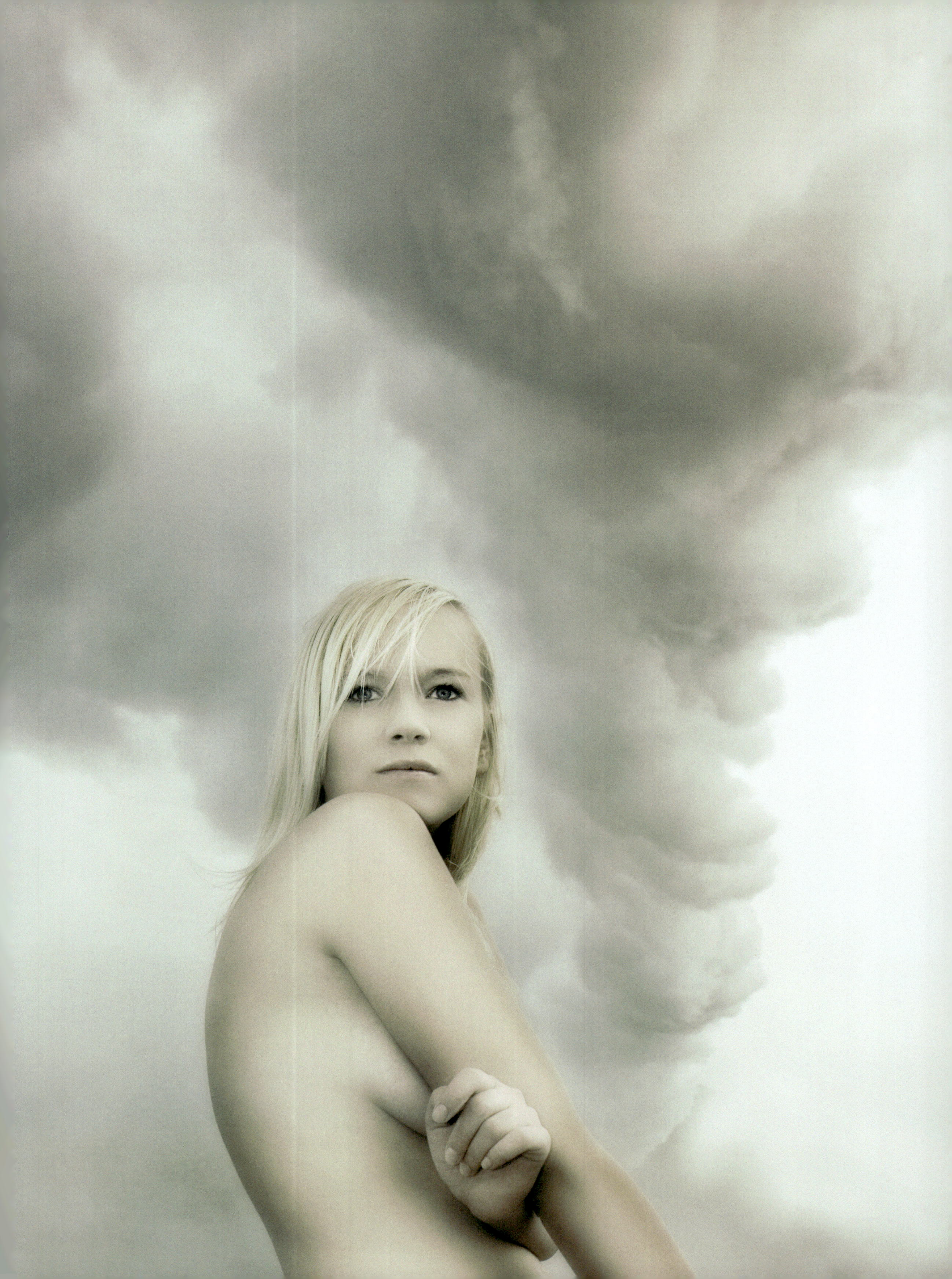

To a stone

My hands
touch you
in veneration

I know
you want me
to caress you with tenderness
and to whisper
words of endearment

I know you want
to feel my nakedness
against your rough skin
to feel how fragile I am
and tender

You shall receive
all you ask for

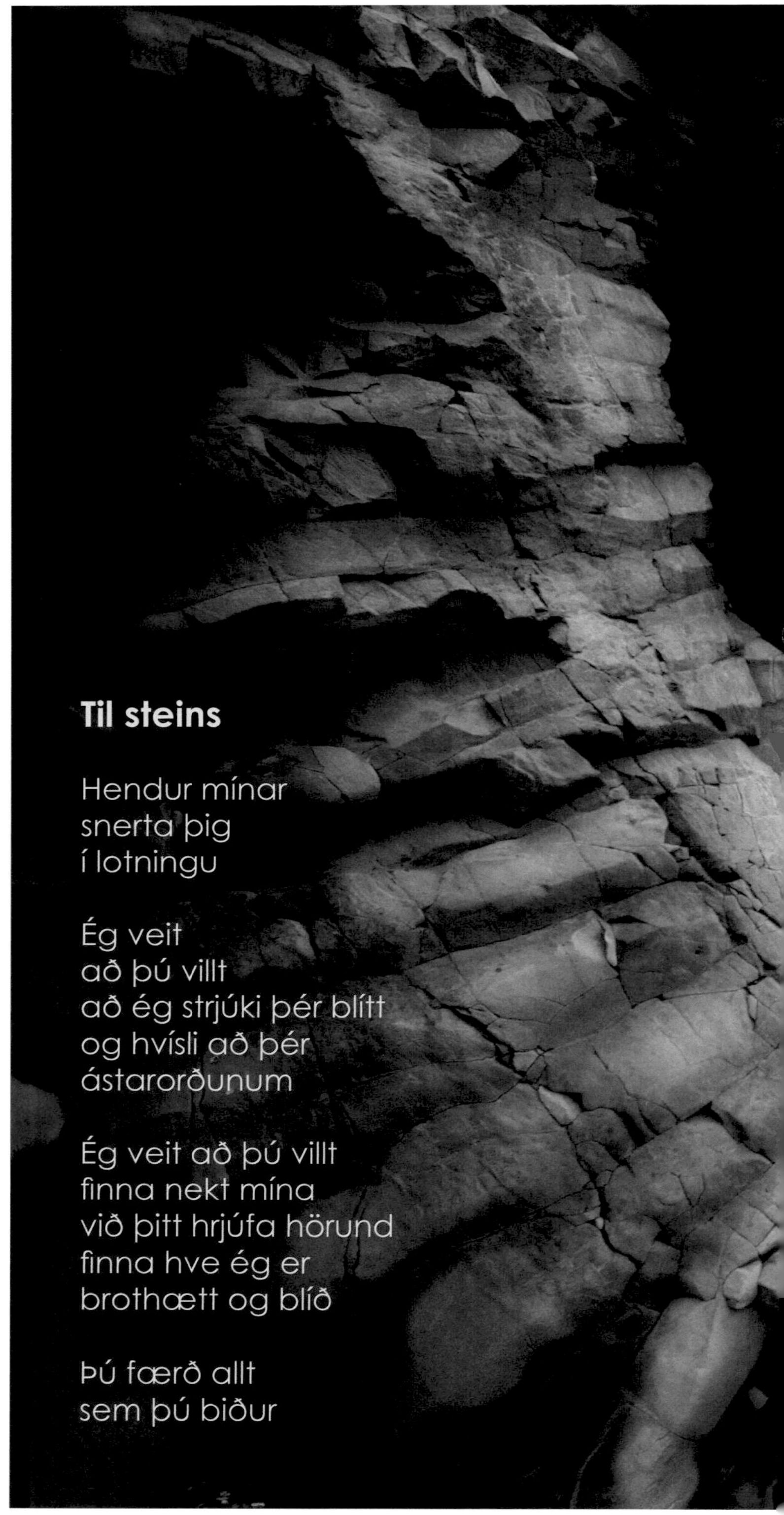

Til steins

Hendur mínar
snerta þig
í lotningu

Ég veit
að þú villt
að ég strjúki þér blítt
og hvísli að þér
ástarorðunum

Ég veit að þú villt
finna nekt mína
við þitt hrjúfa hörund
finna hve ég er
brothætt og blíð

Þú færð allt
sem þú biður

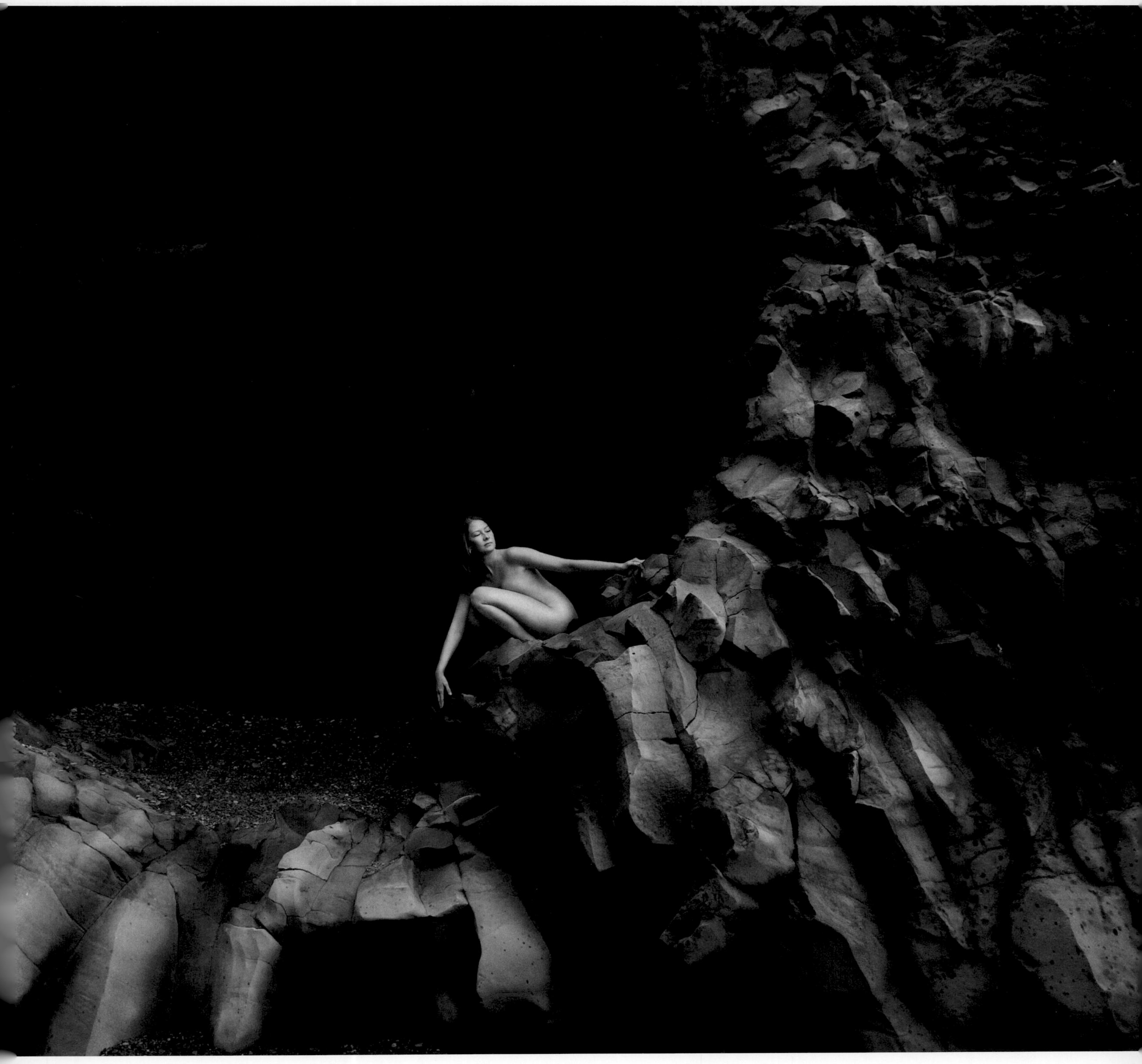

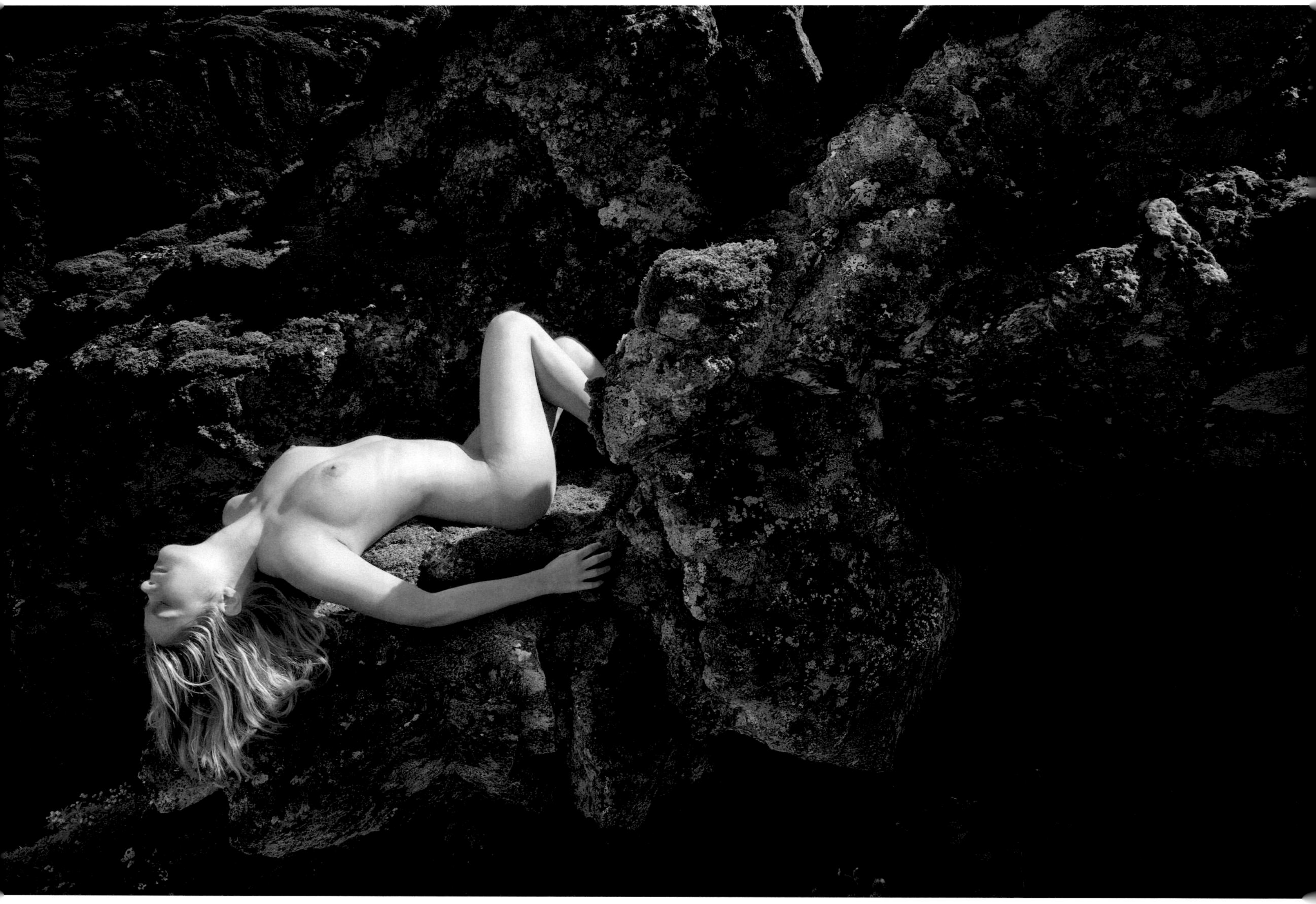

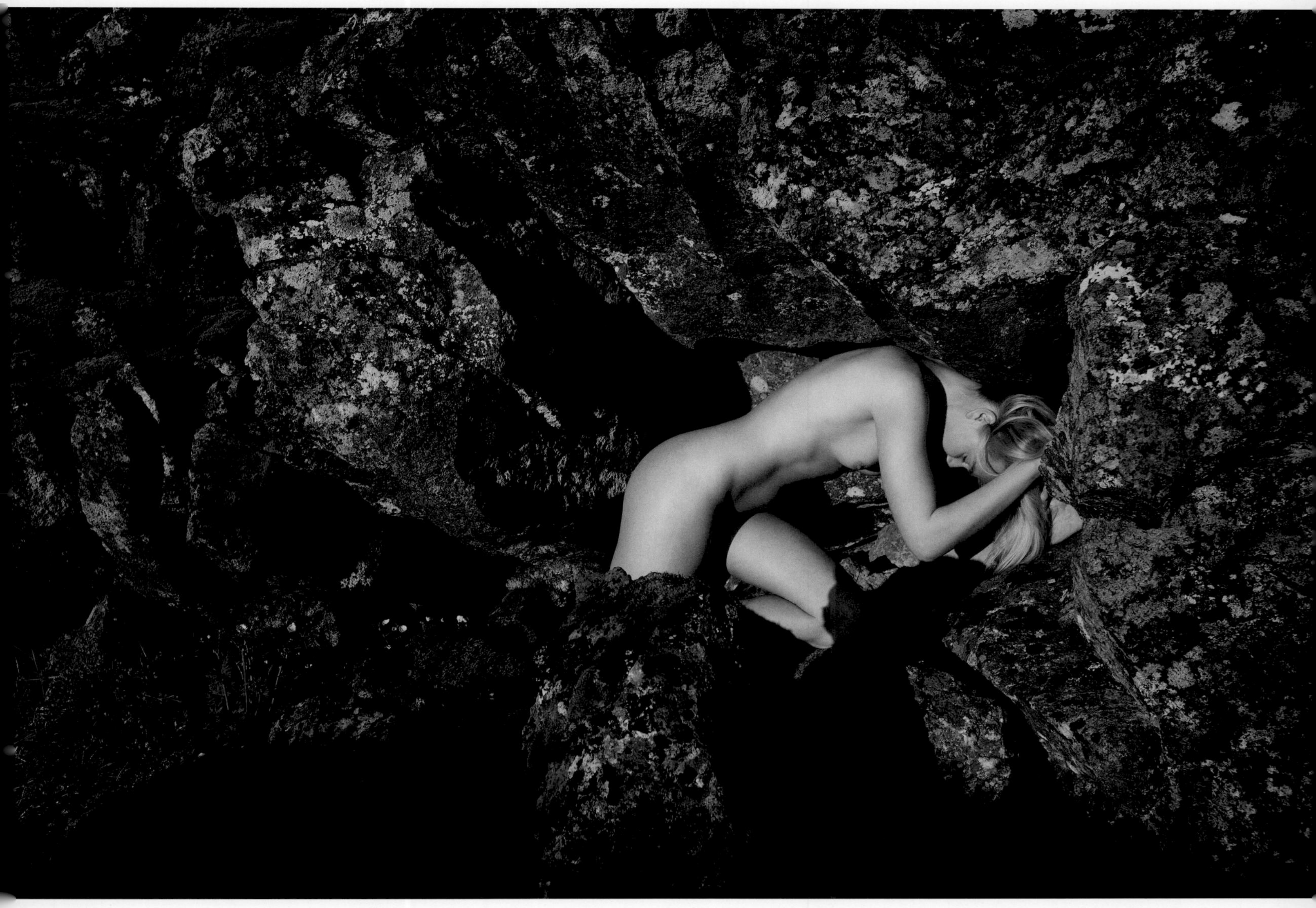

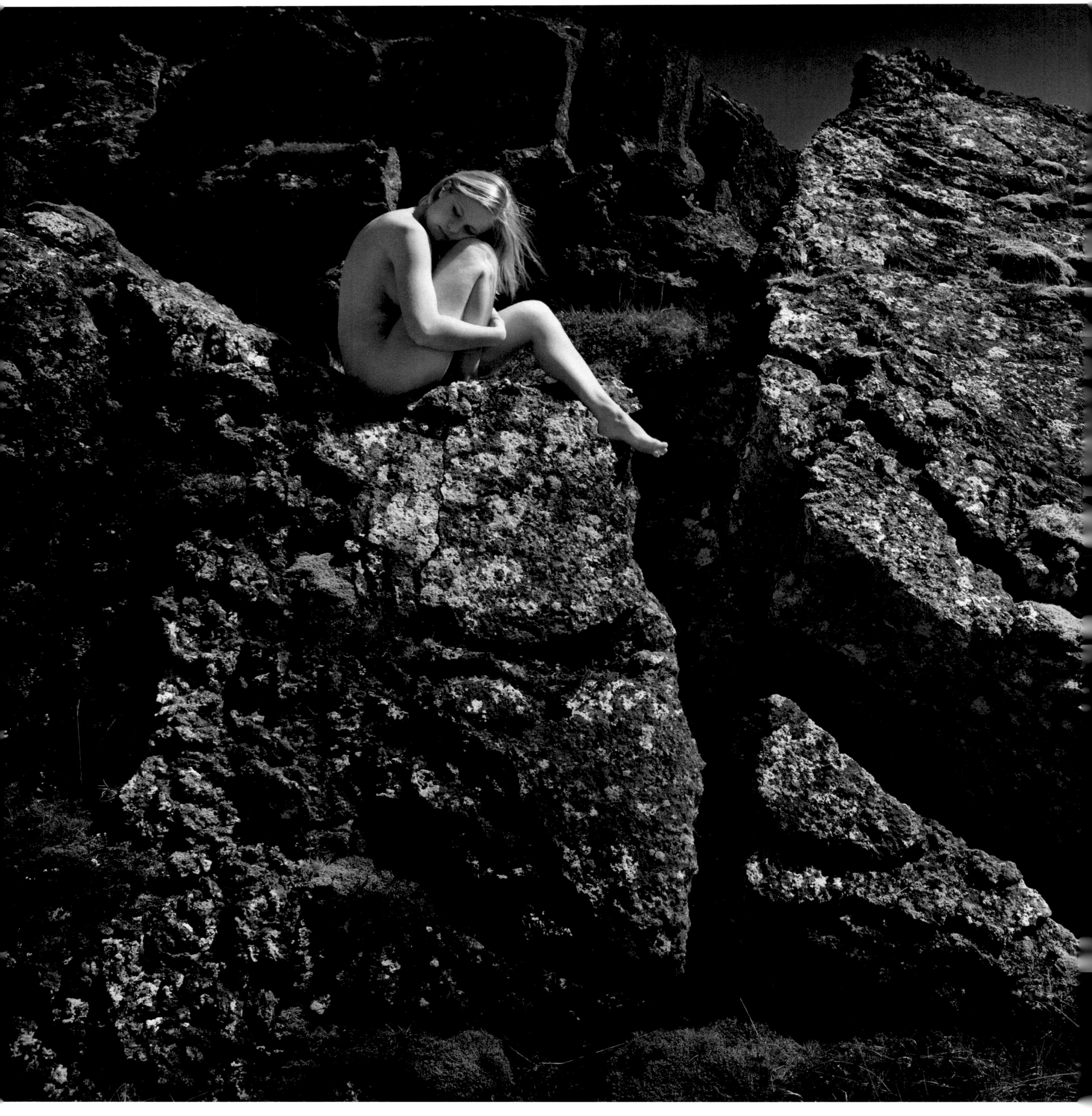

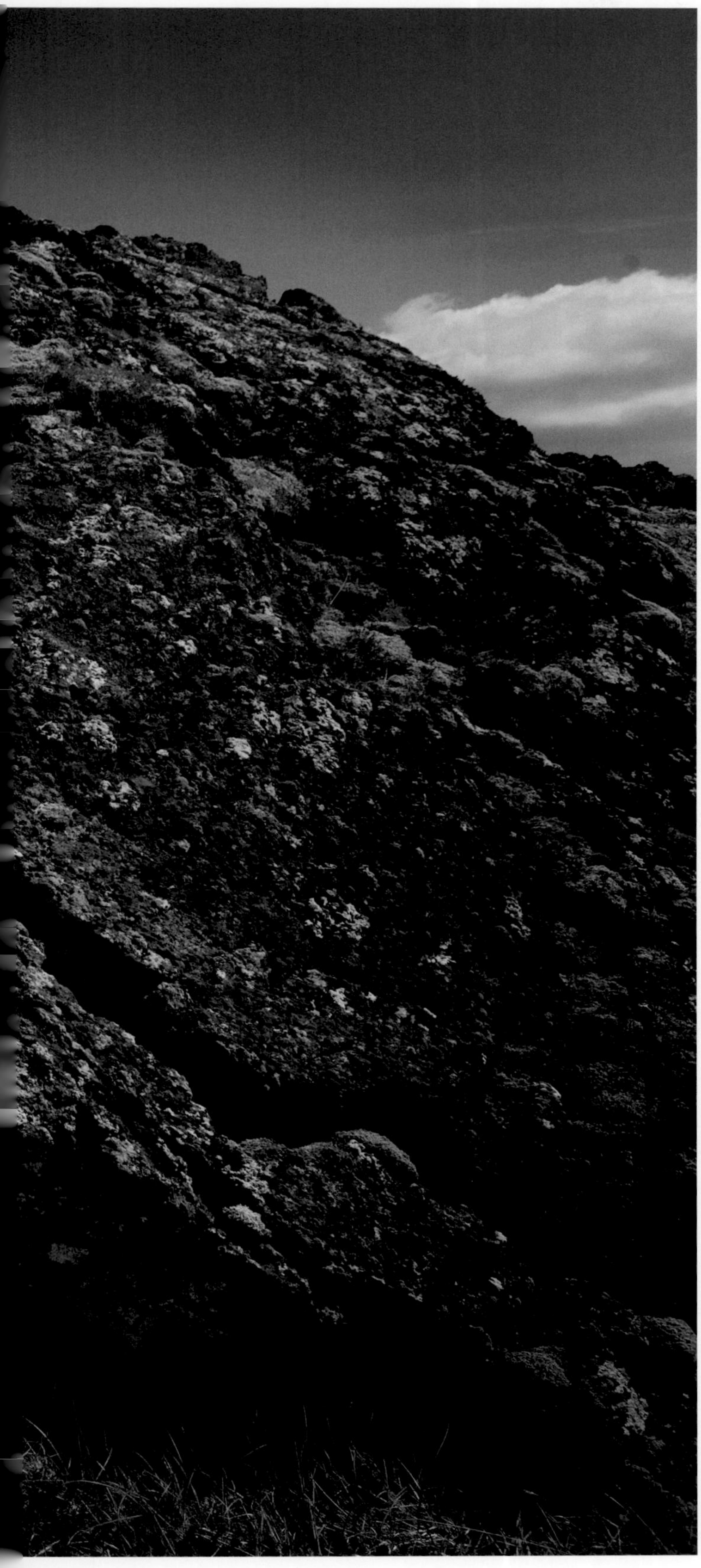

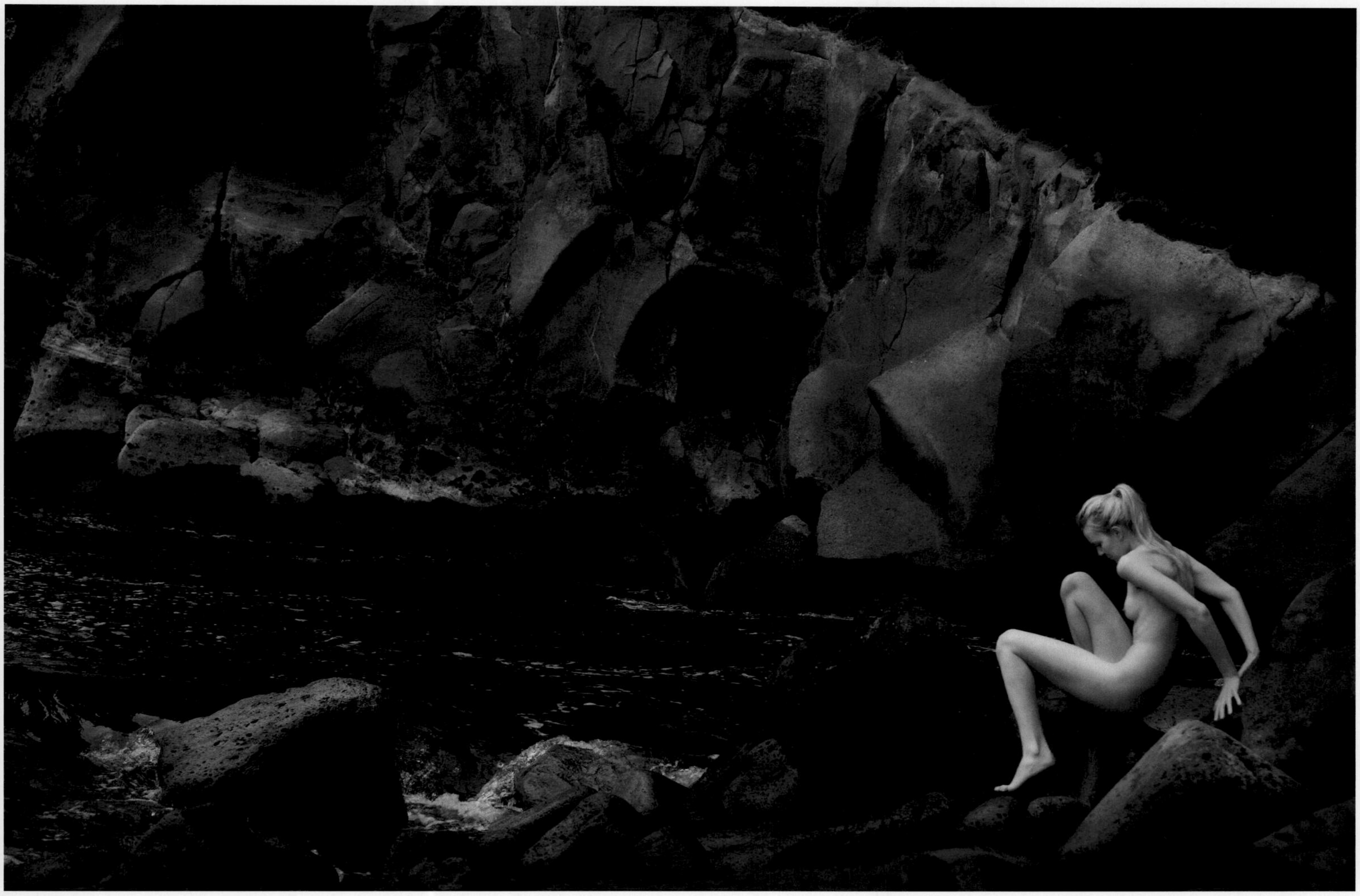

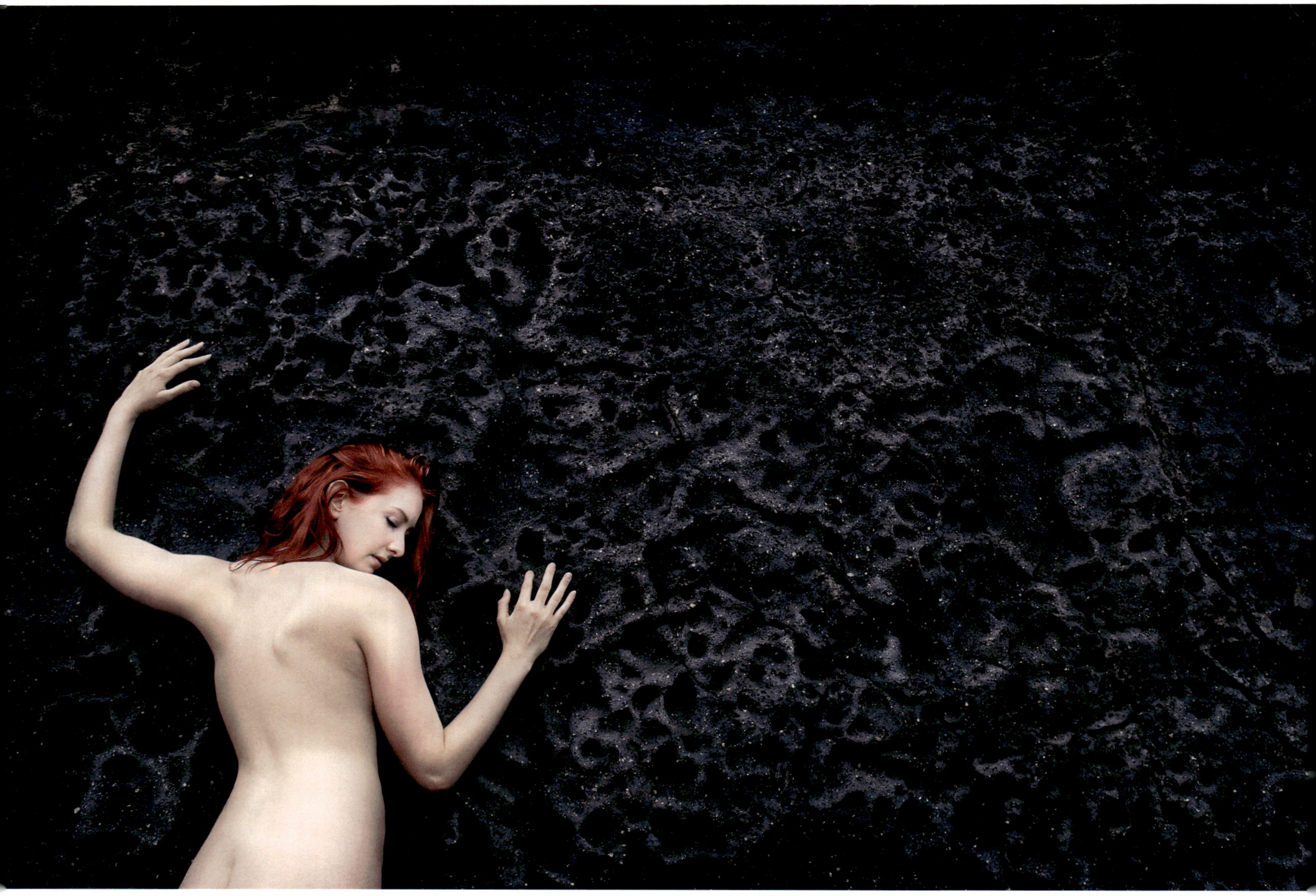

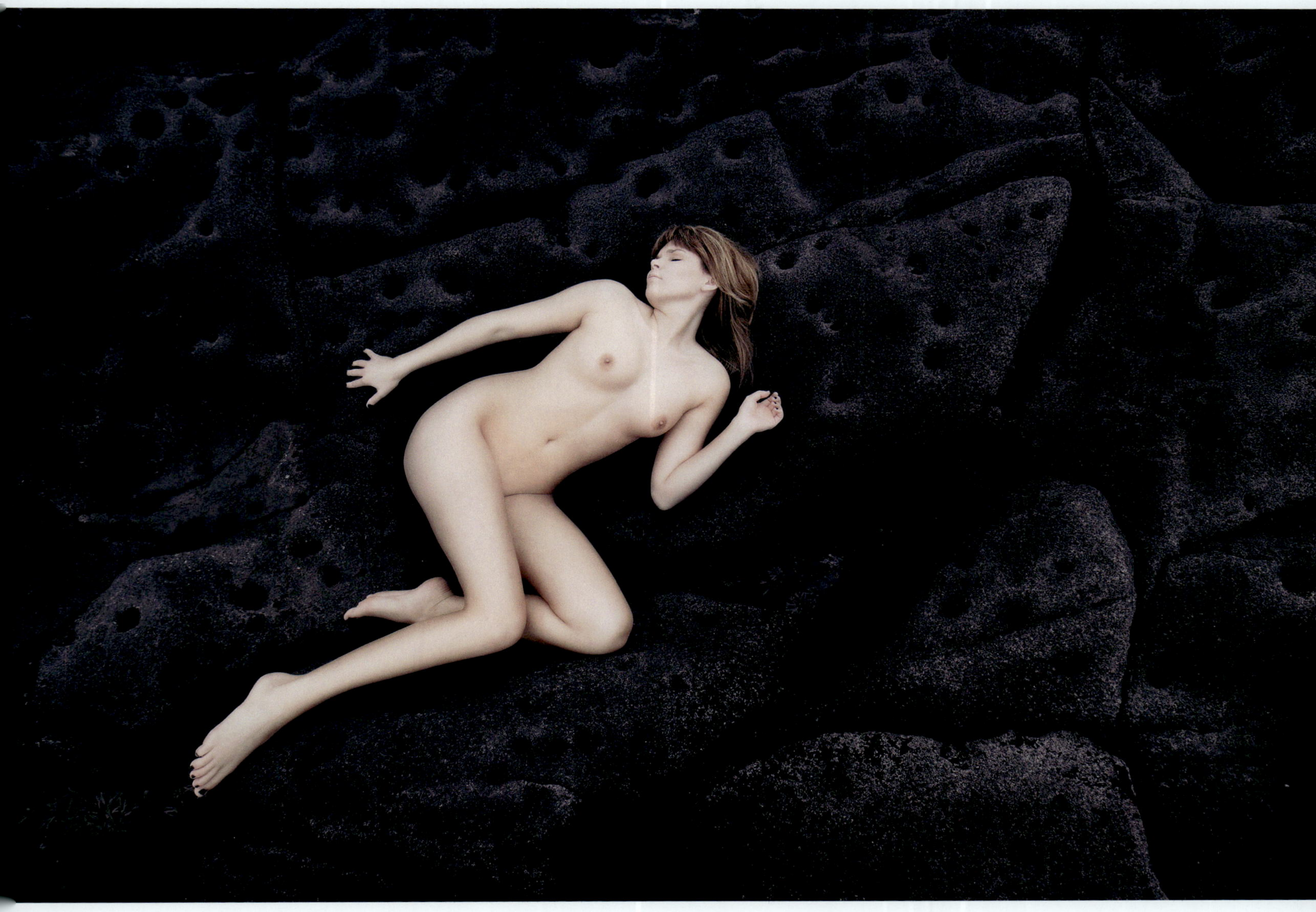

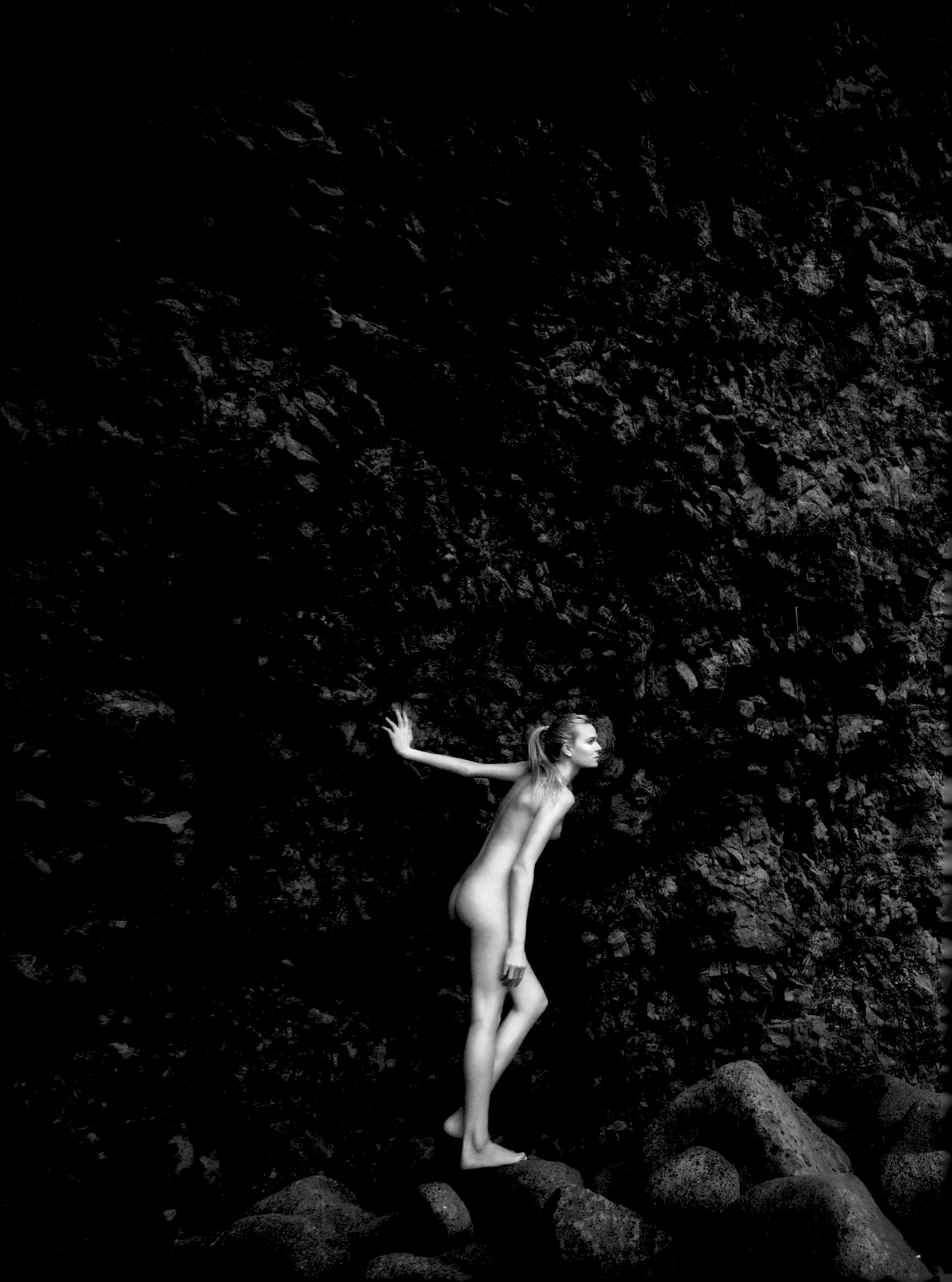

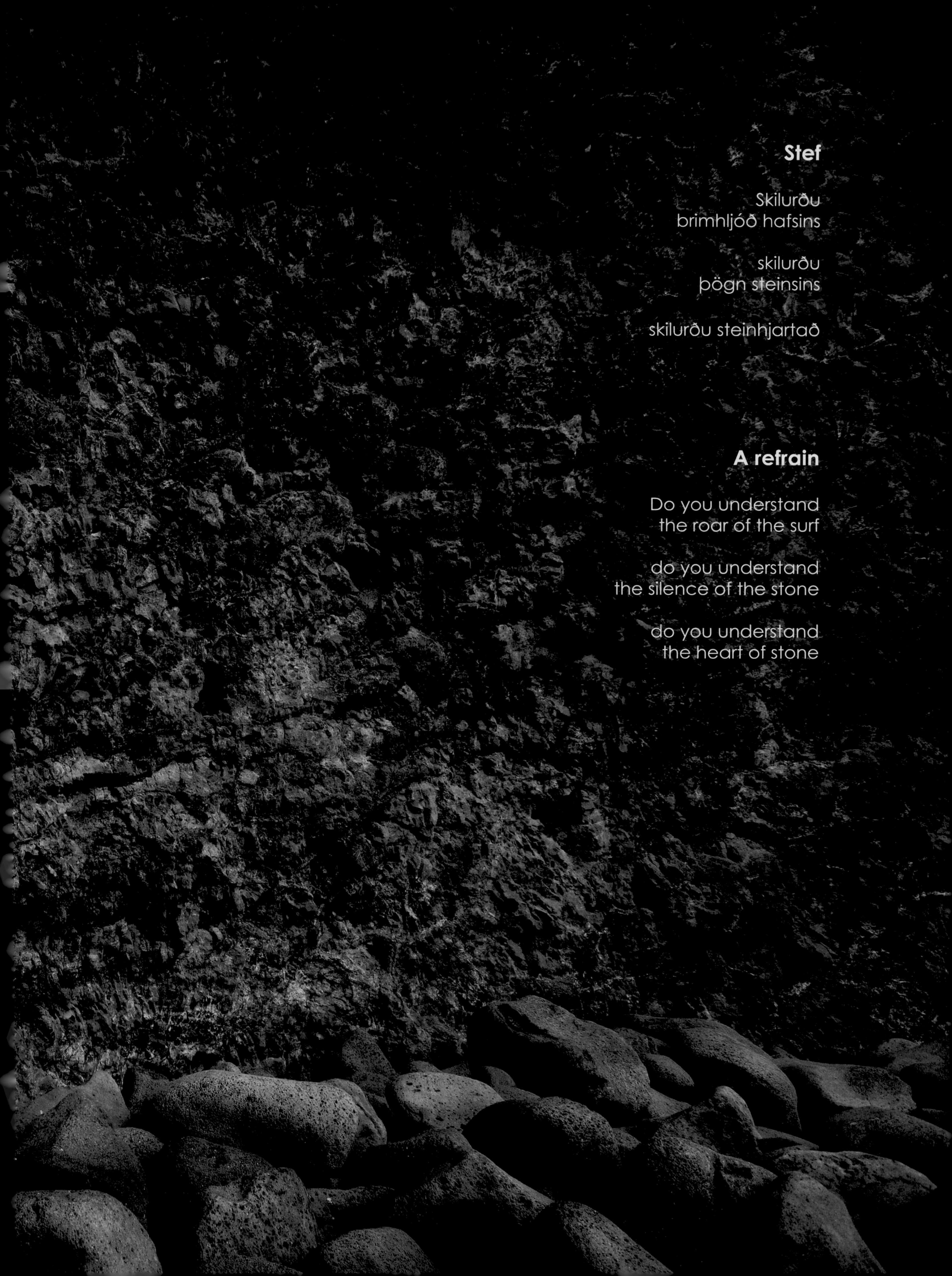

Stef

Skilurðu
brimhljóð hafsins

skilurðu
þögn steinsins

skilurðu steinhjartað

A refrain

Do you understand
the roar of the surf

do you understand
the silence of the stone

do you understand
the heart of stone

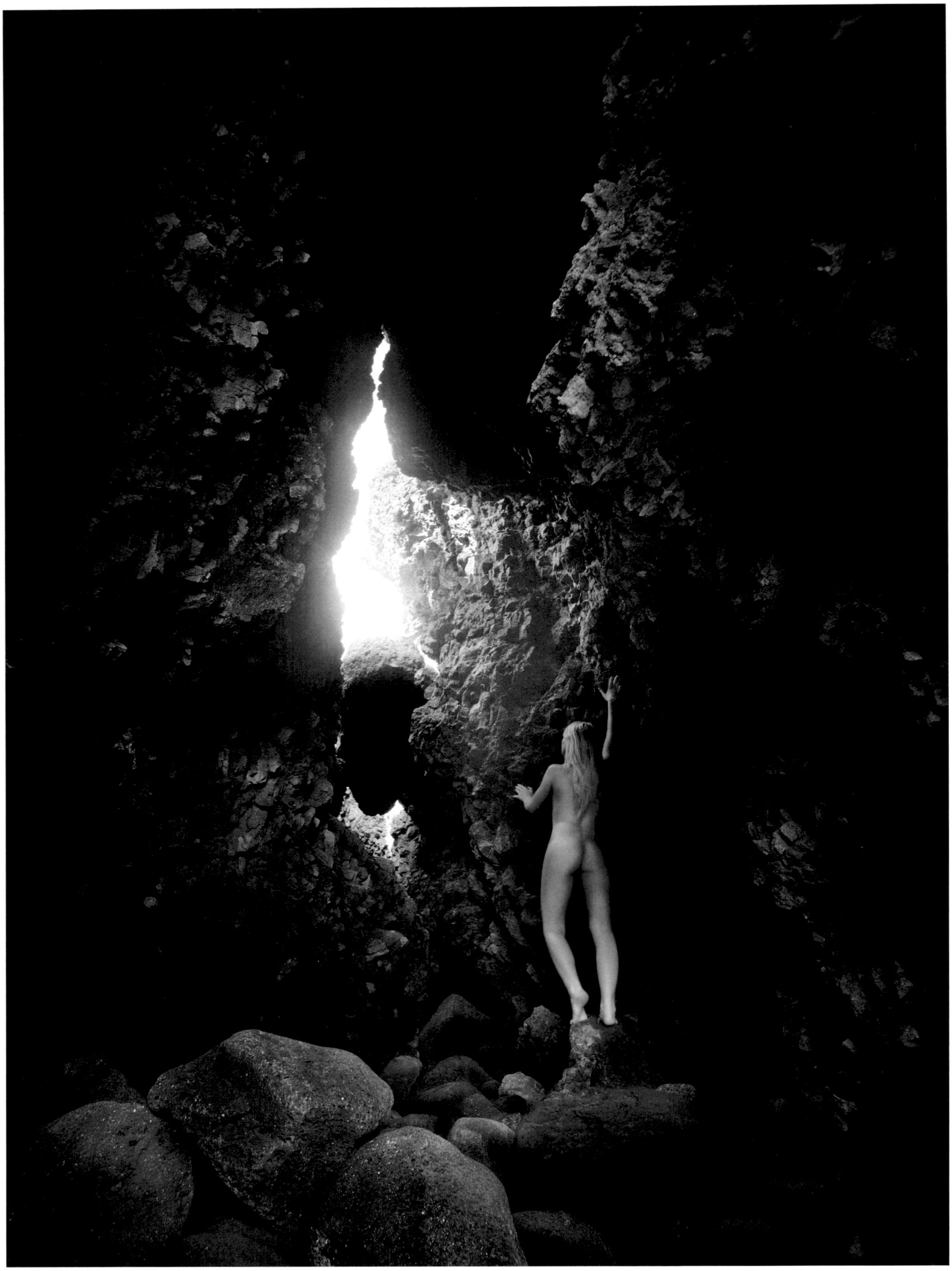

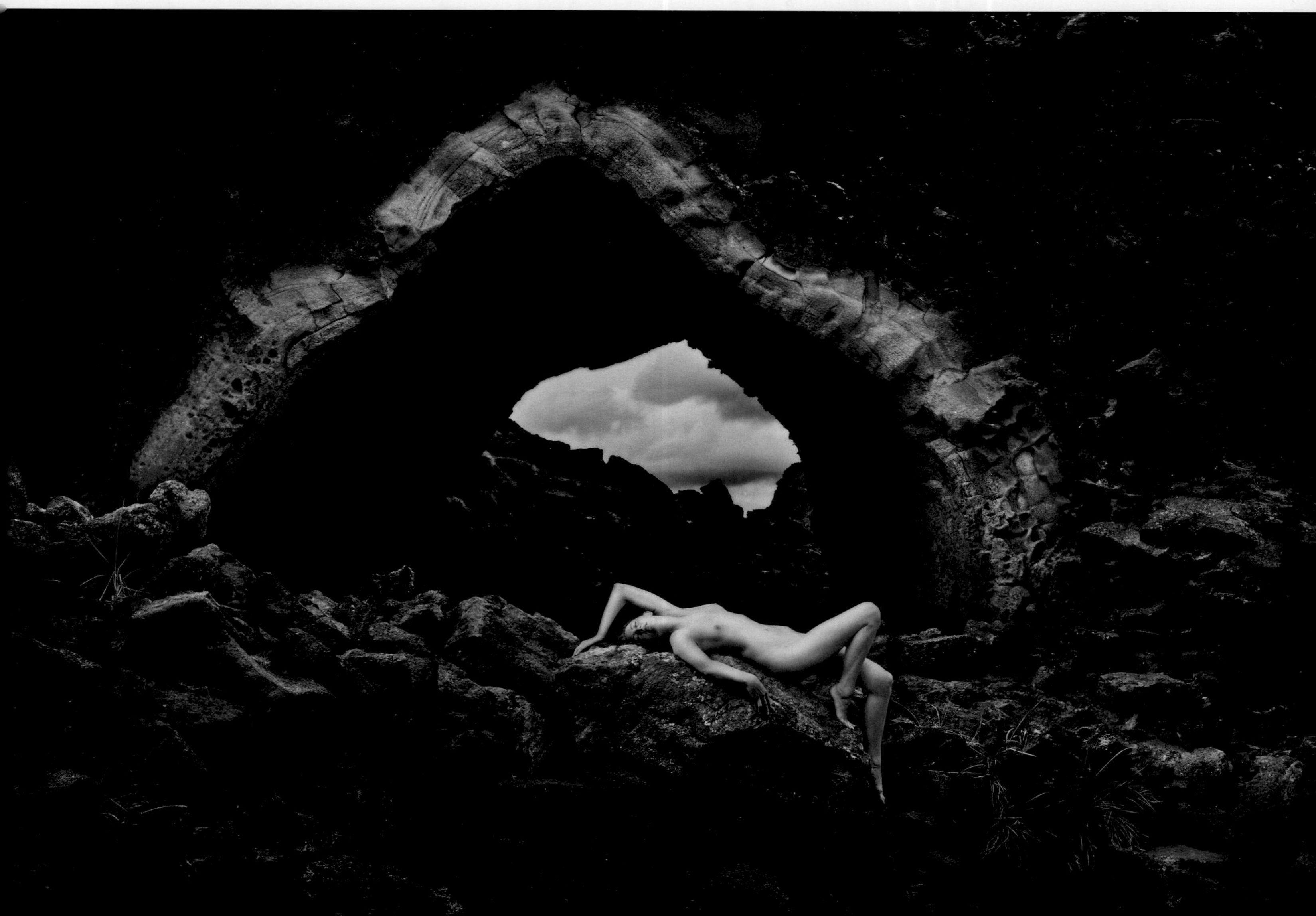

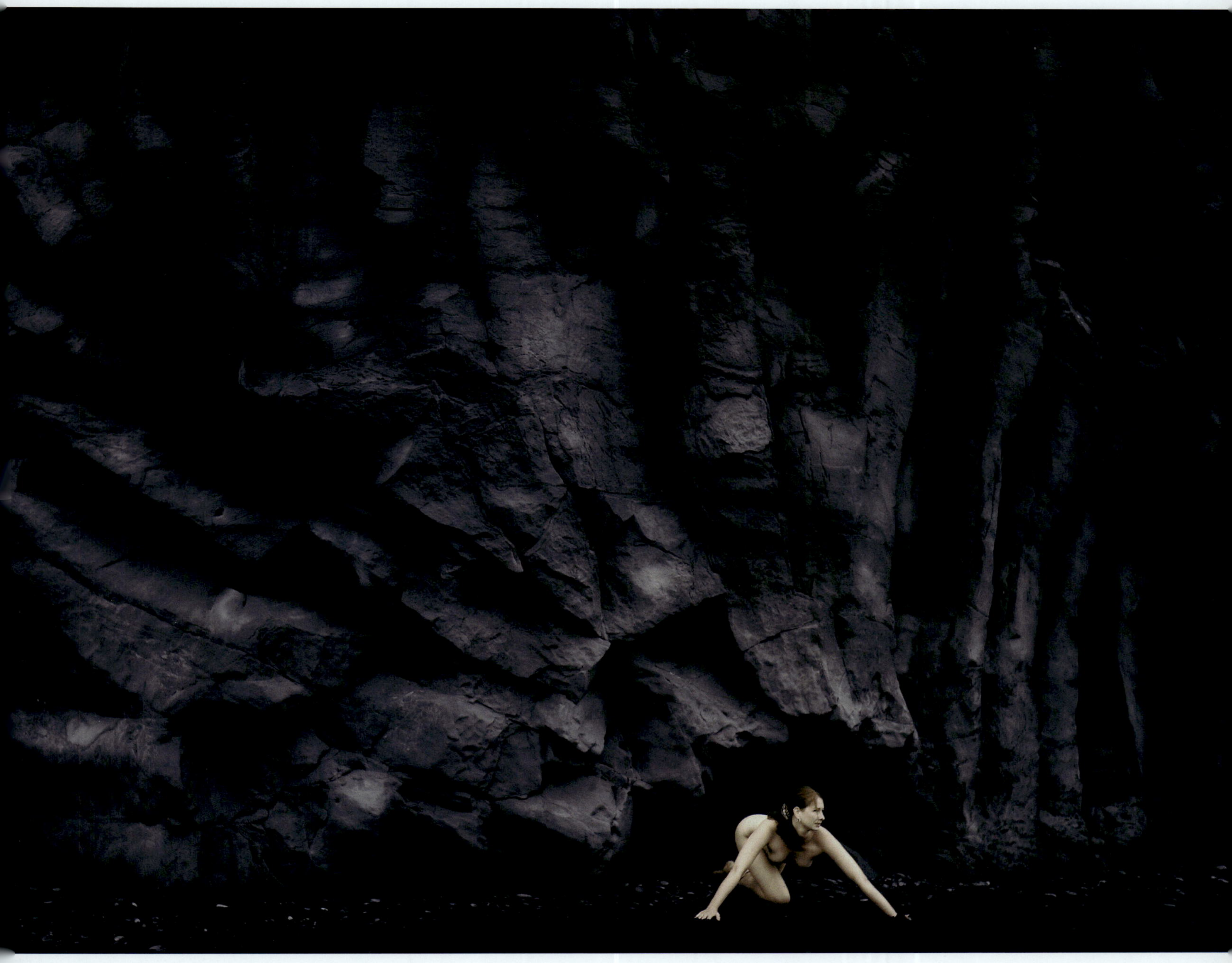

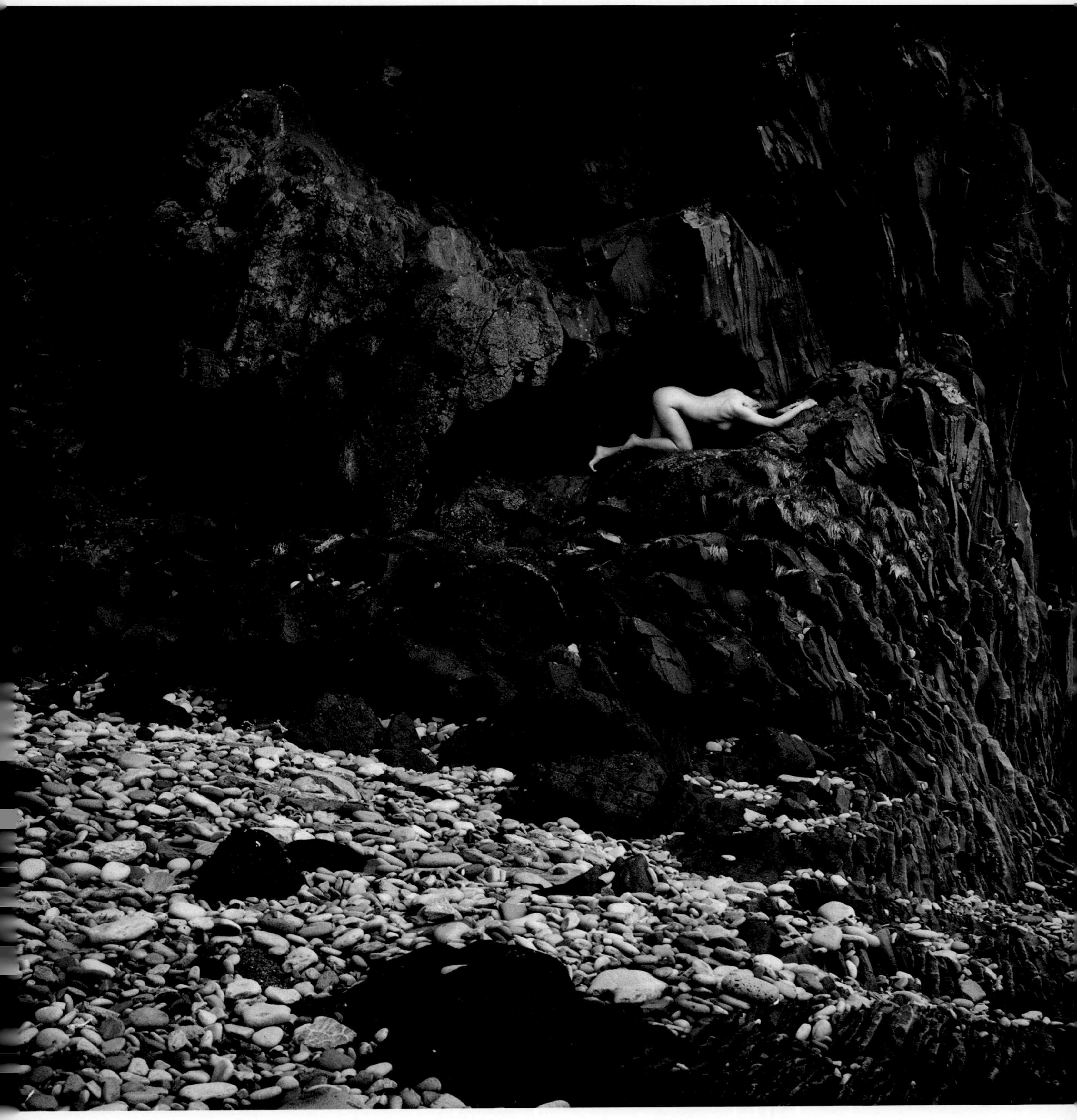

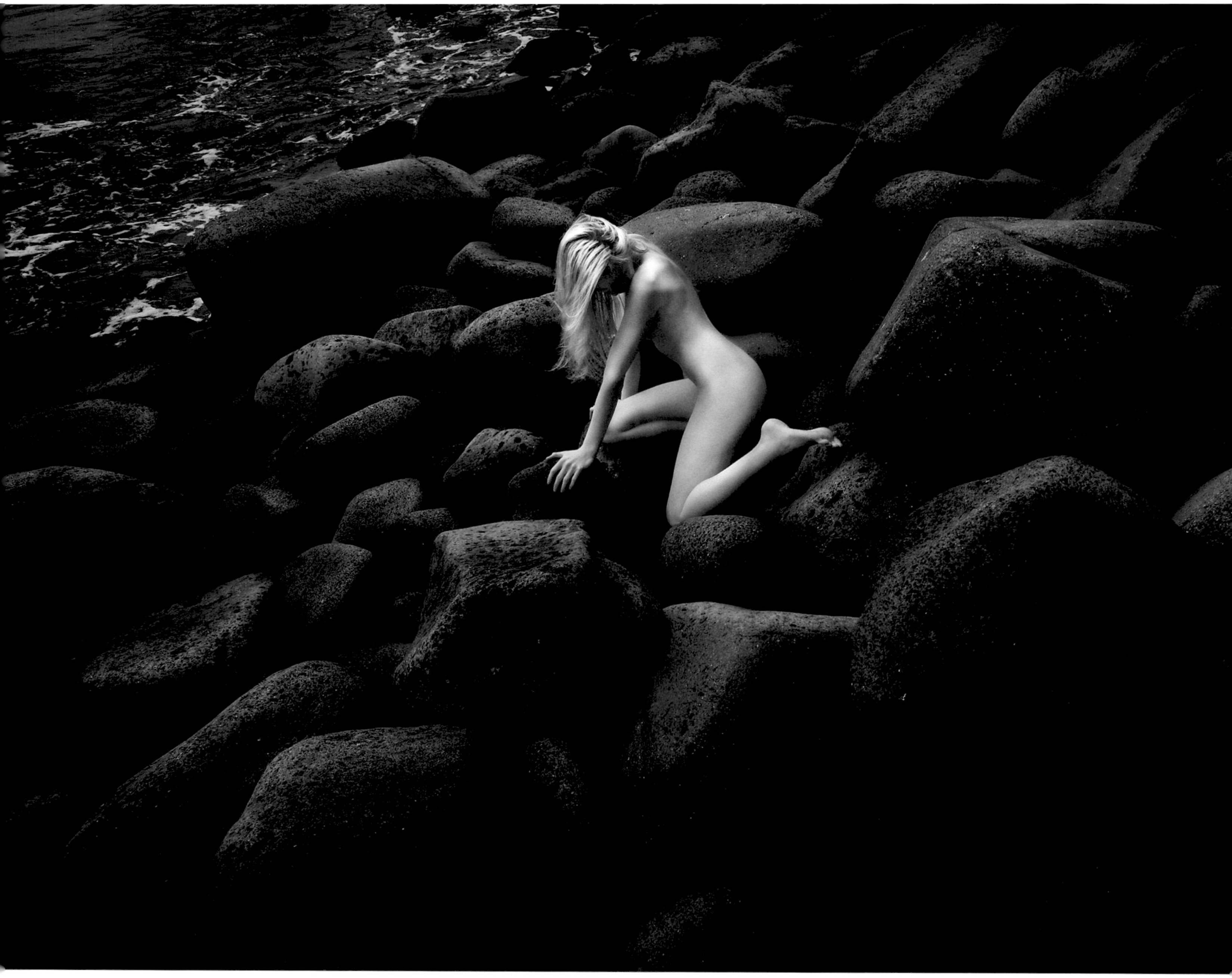

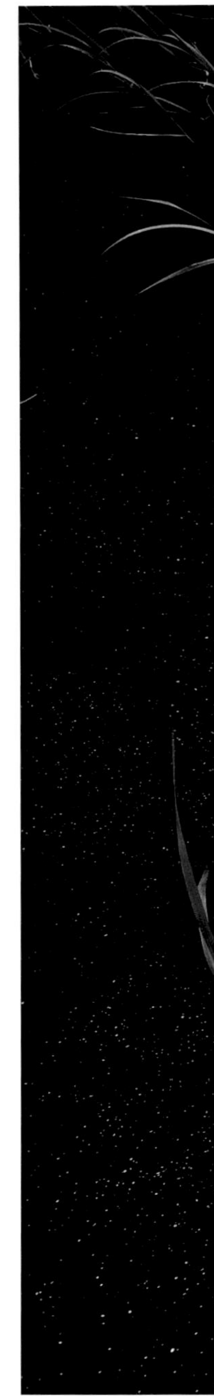

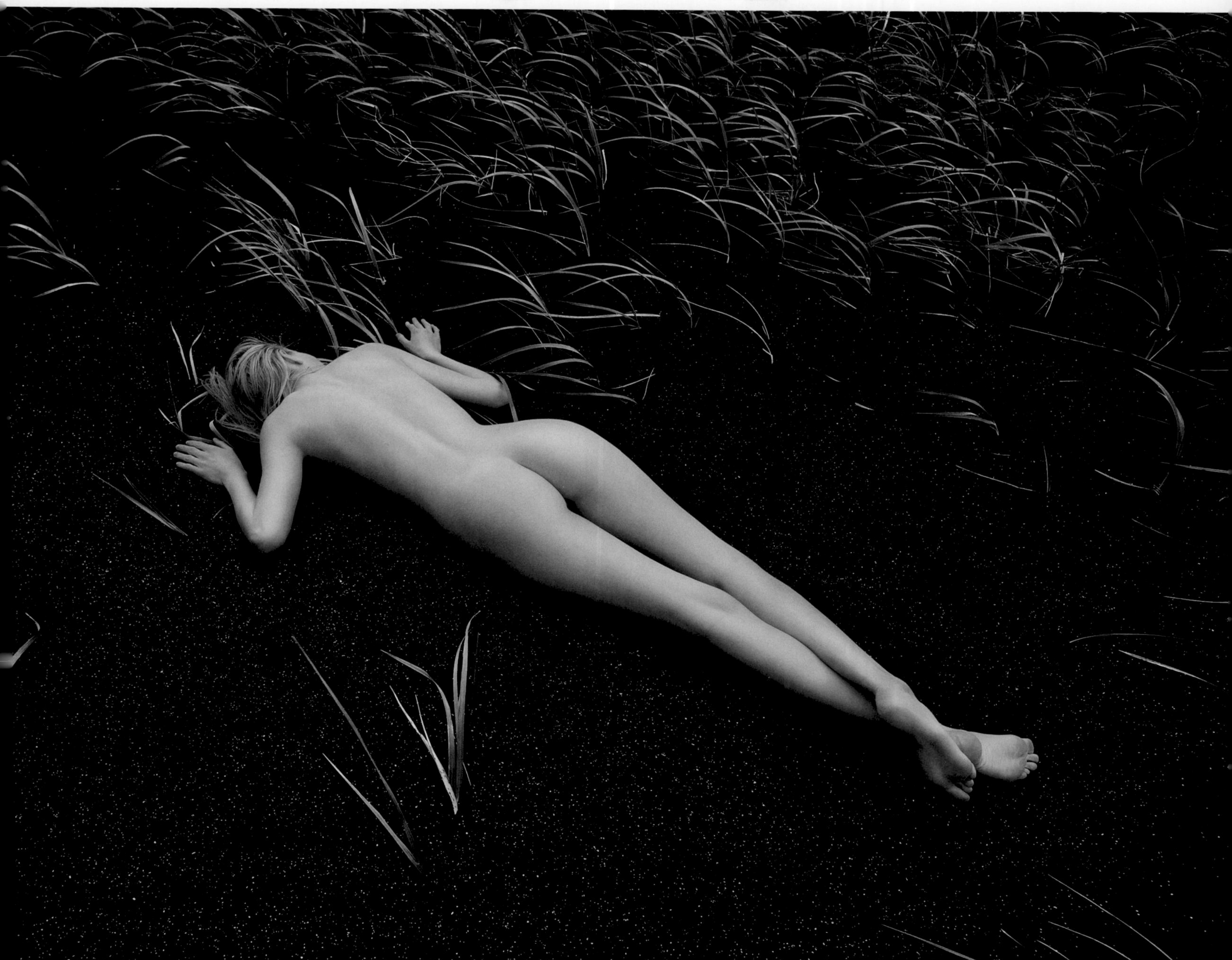

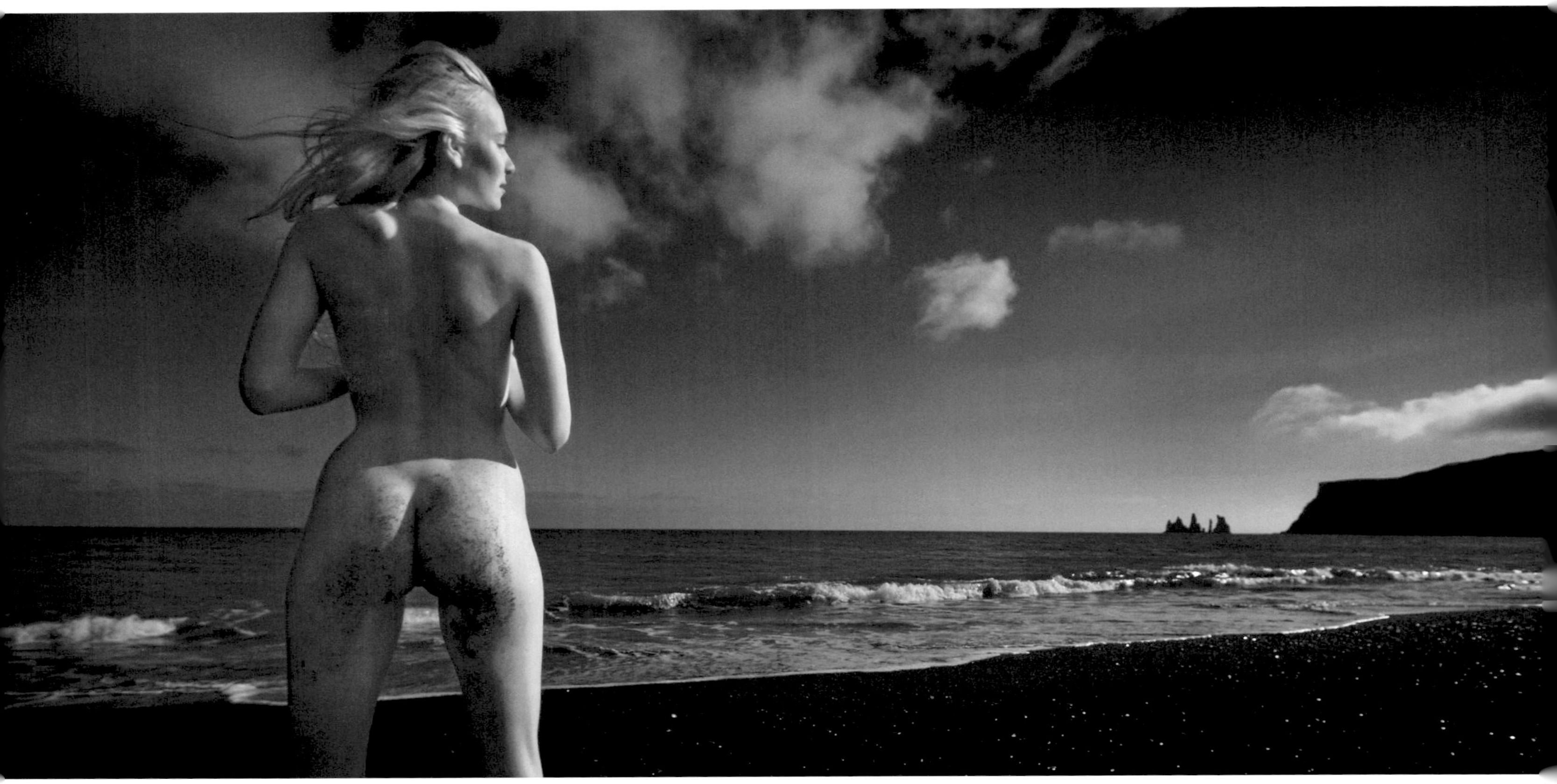

Ferðalag

Hægur blær
hafsins
snertir kinn þína
blíðlega
augu þín brenna
Hann getur ekki dvalið lengi
heldur för sinni áfram
Ef þú vilt ekki missa af honum
verðurðu að fylgja honum eftir
niður að strönd
yfir hafið
verða að hægum blæ
sem snertir kinn einhvers
blíðlega
Getur ekki dvalið lengi
ef þú vilt ekki missa af honum
verðurðu að fylgja honum eftir

The journey

Gentle breeze
from the sea
touches you tenderly
on your cheek
your eyes are burning
It cannot stay long
keeps going its way
If you don't want to lose it
you have to follow
to the shore
over the sea
become a gentle breeze
which touches someone tenderly
on his cheek
Cannot stay long
If you don't want to lose it
you have to follow

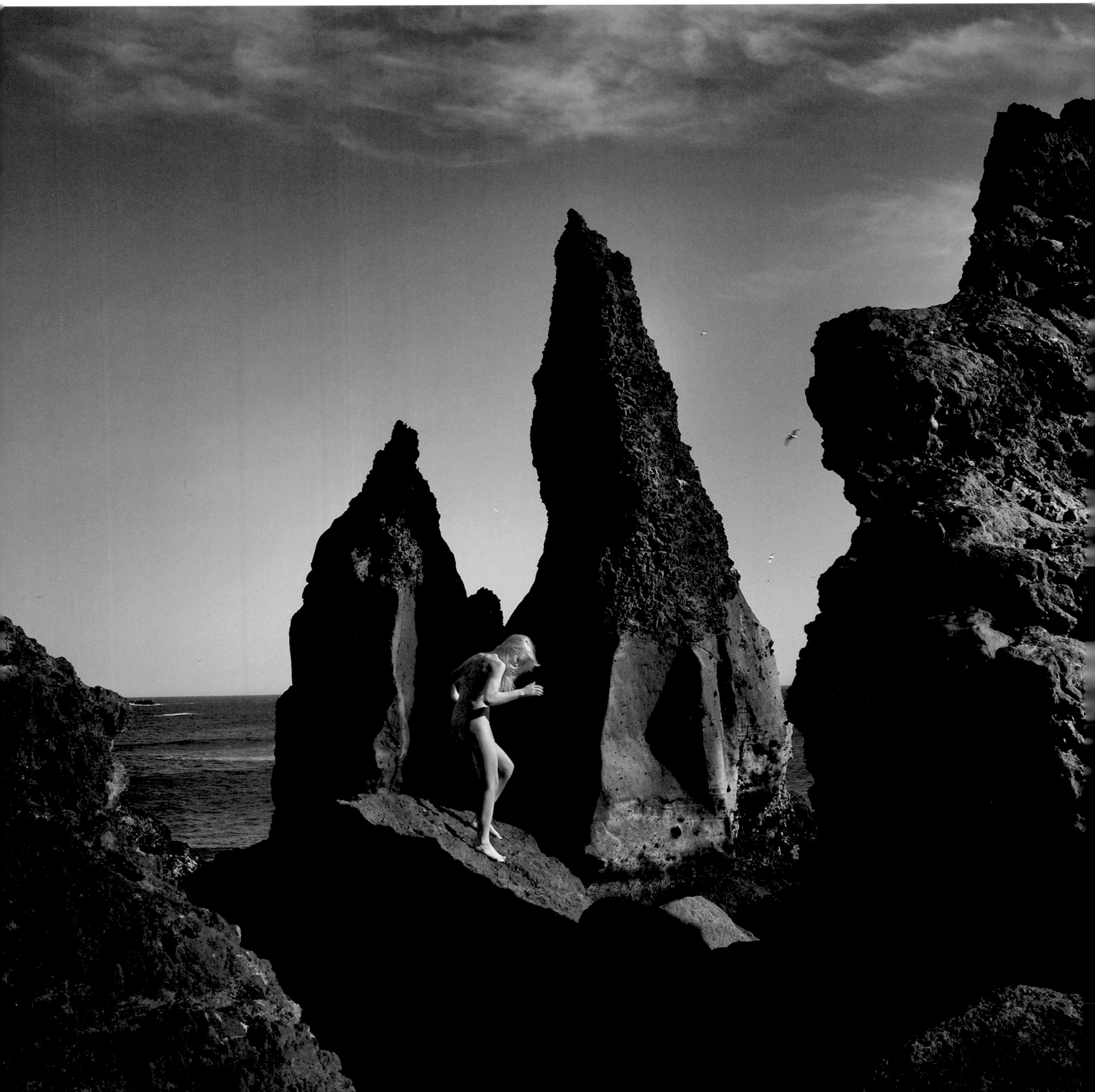

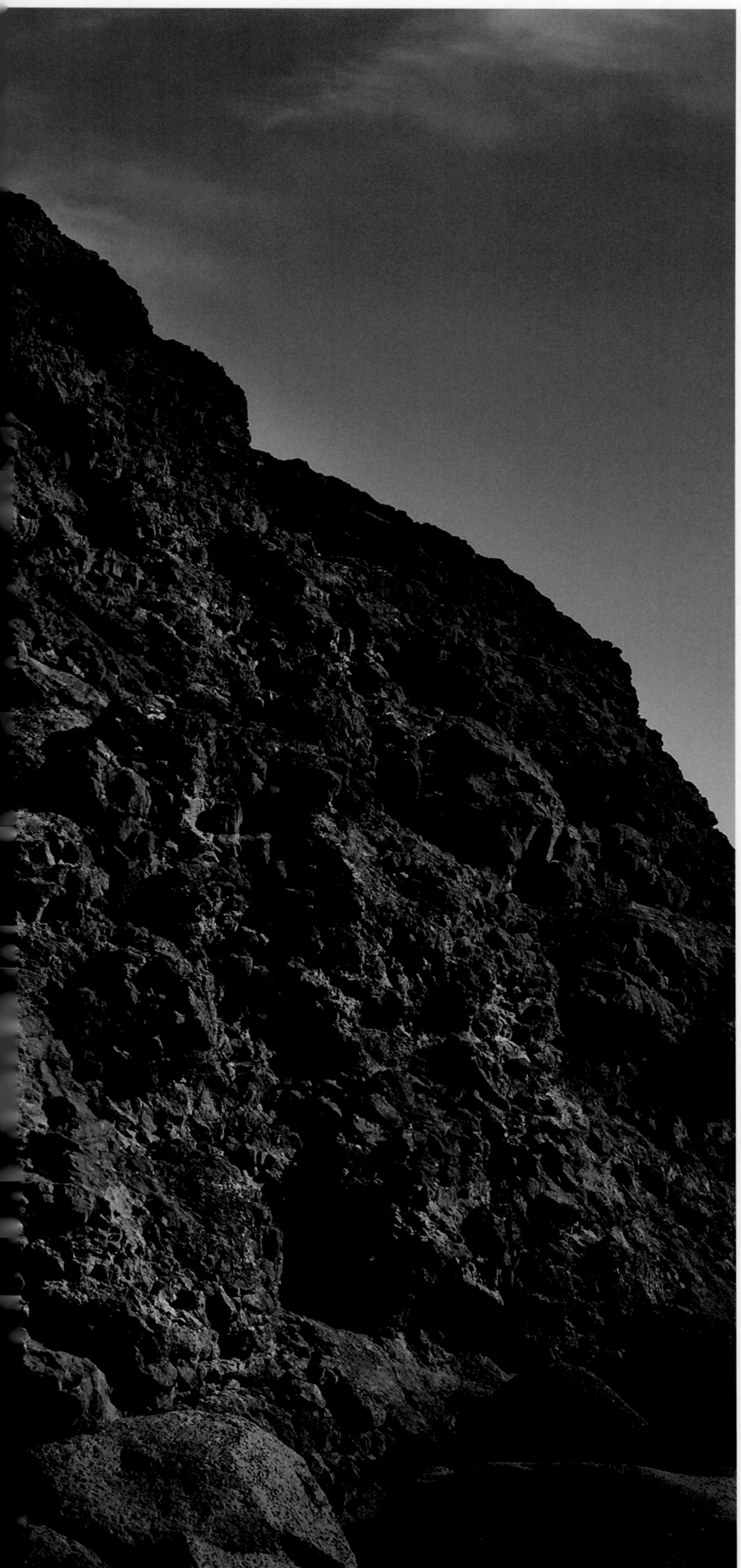

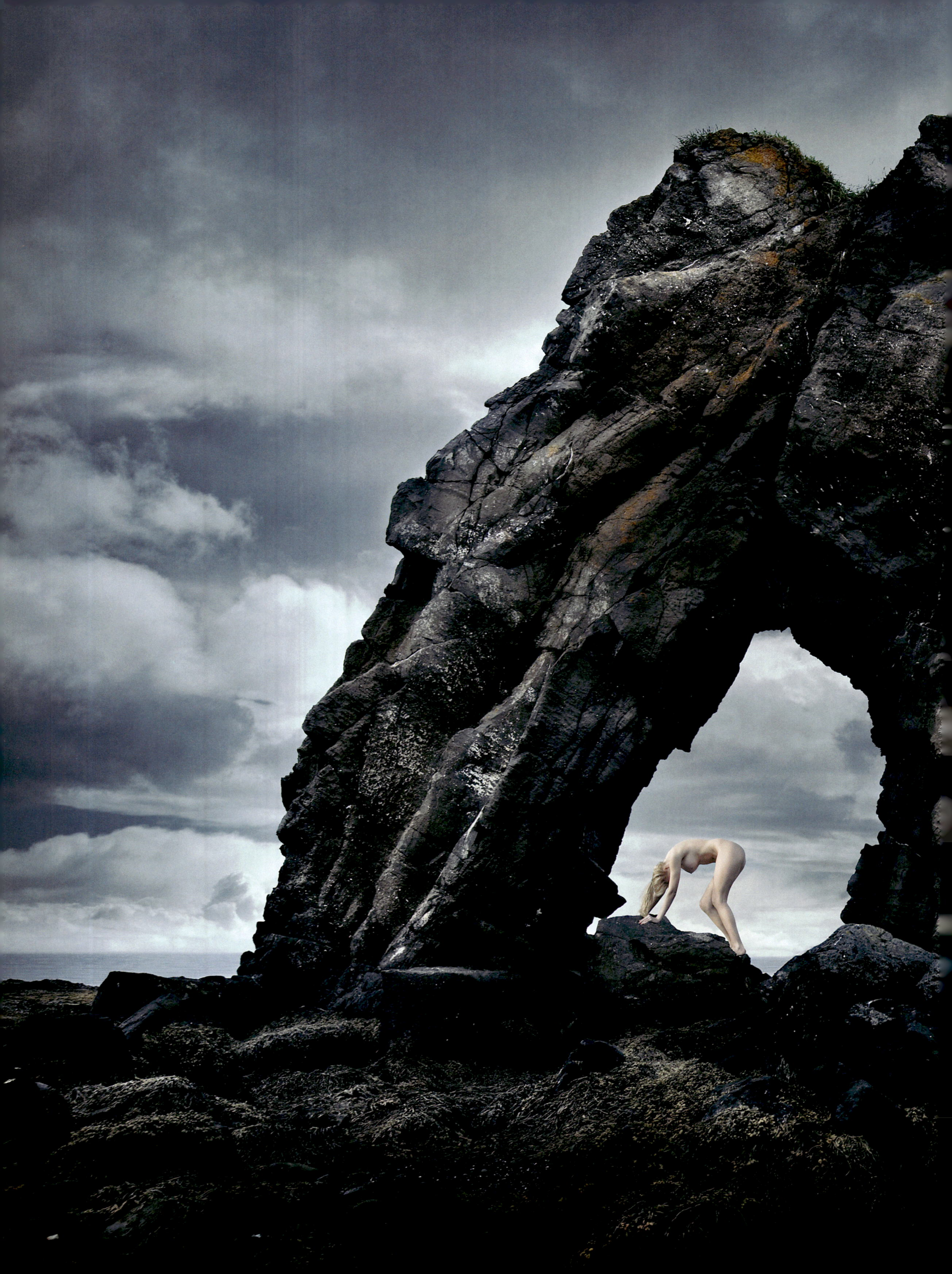

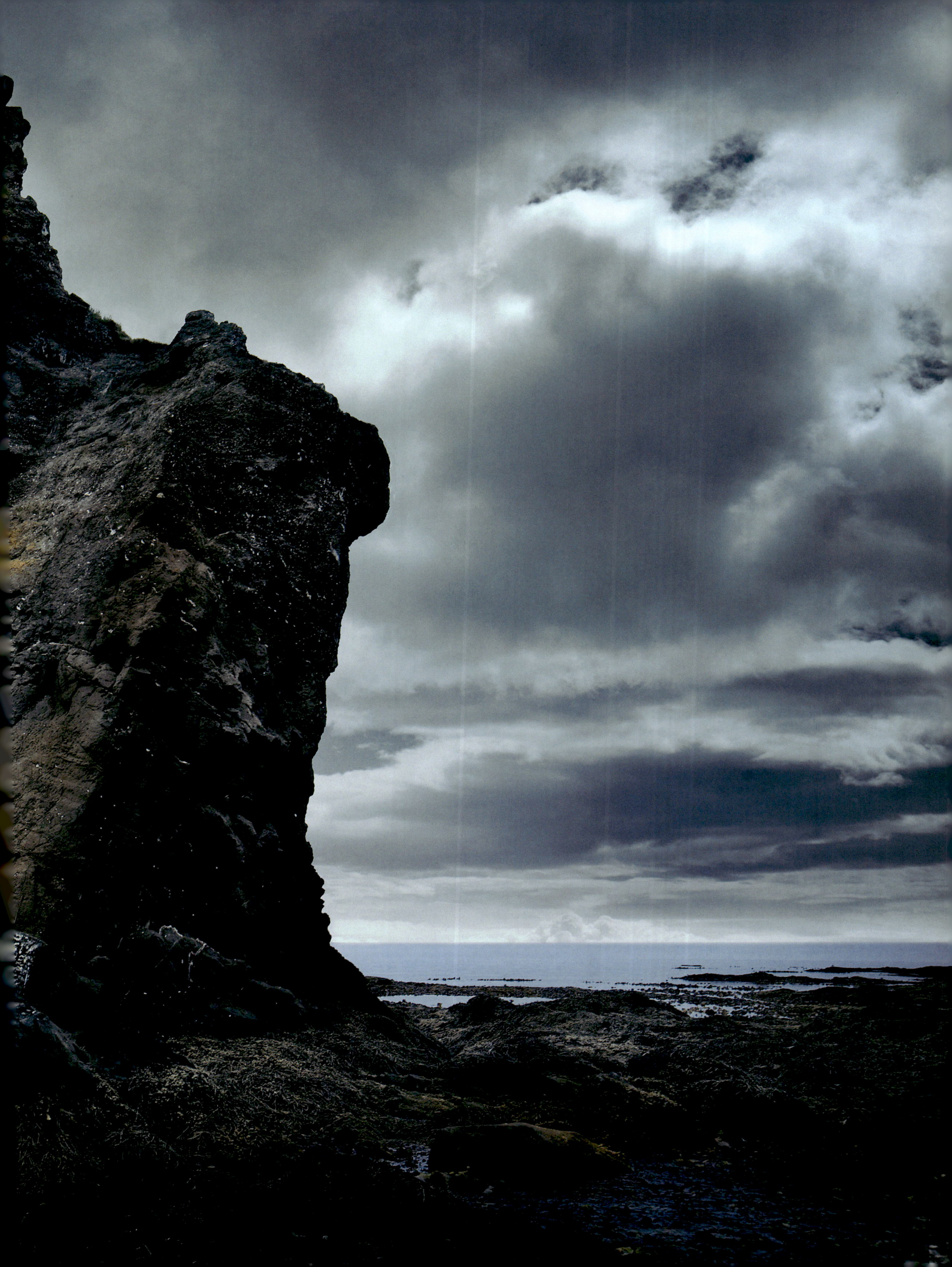

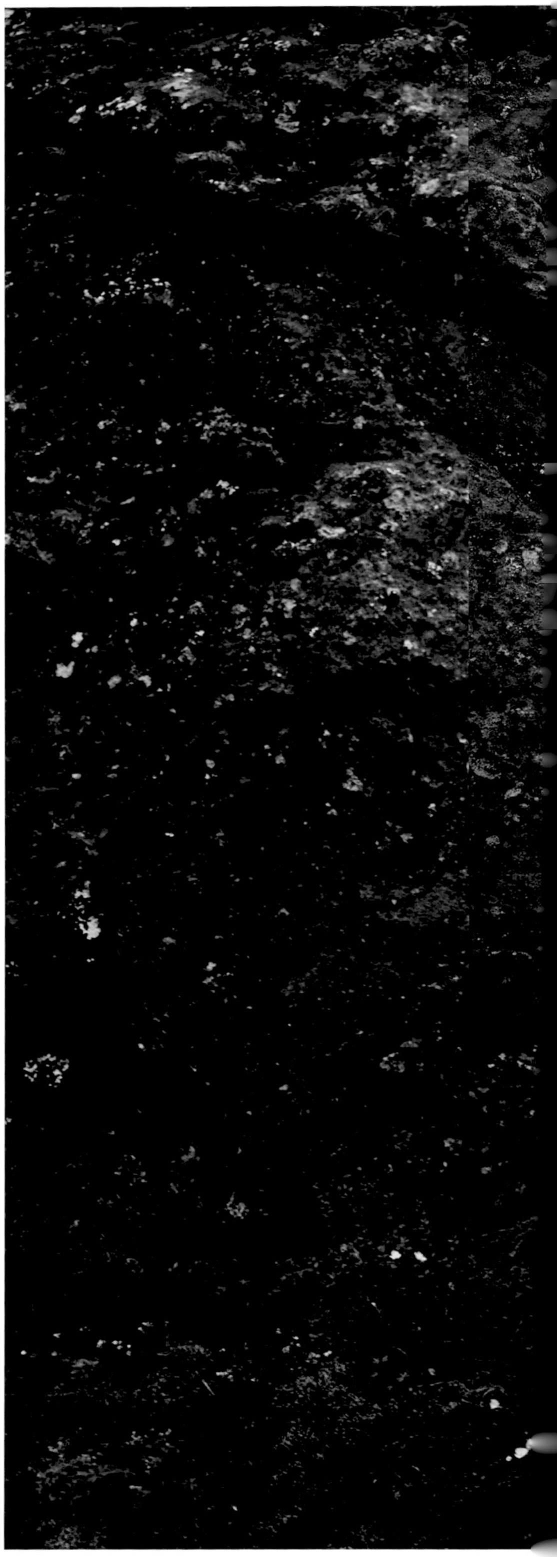

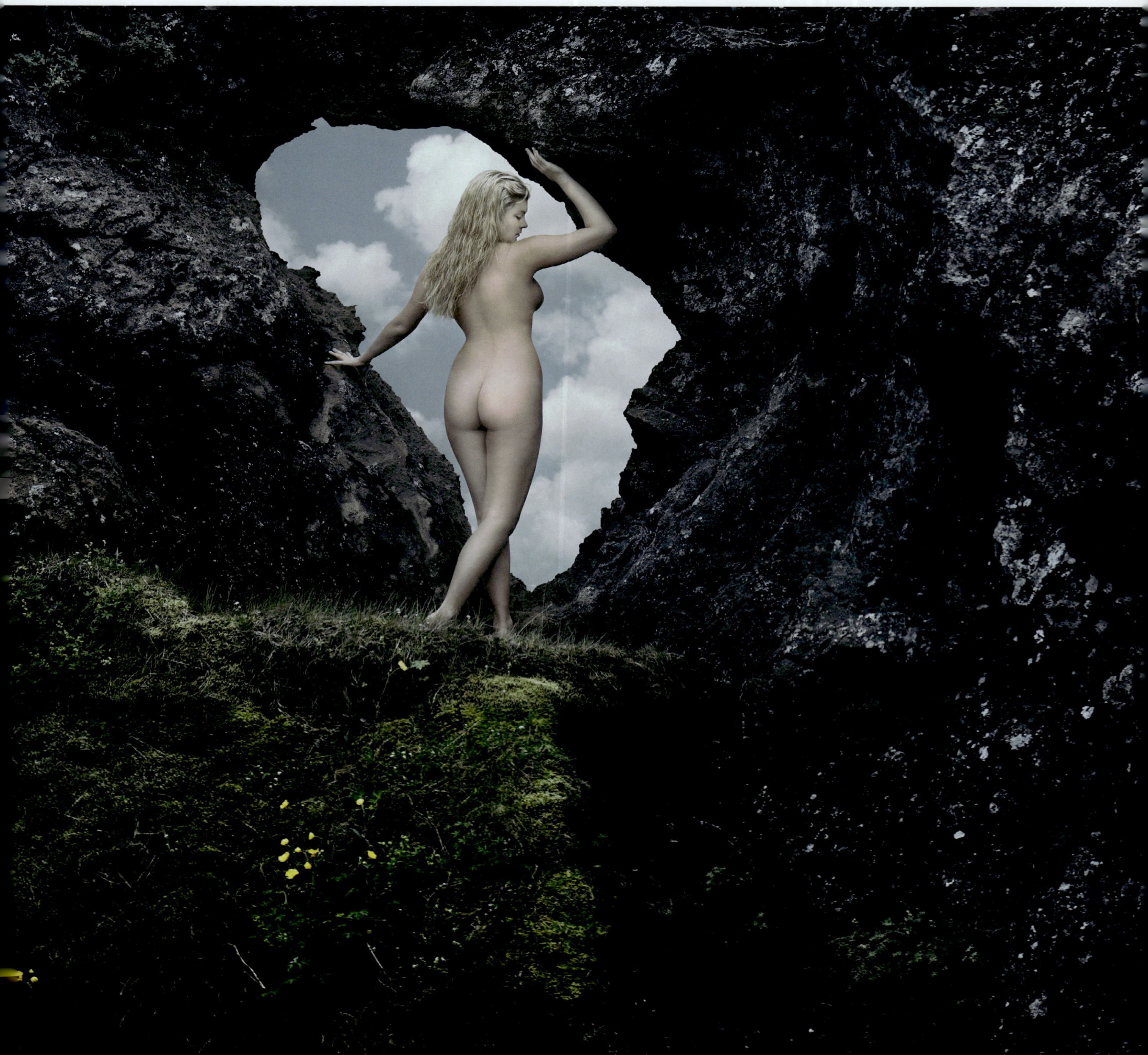

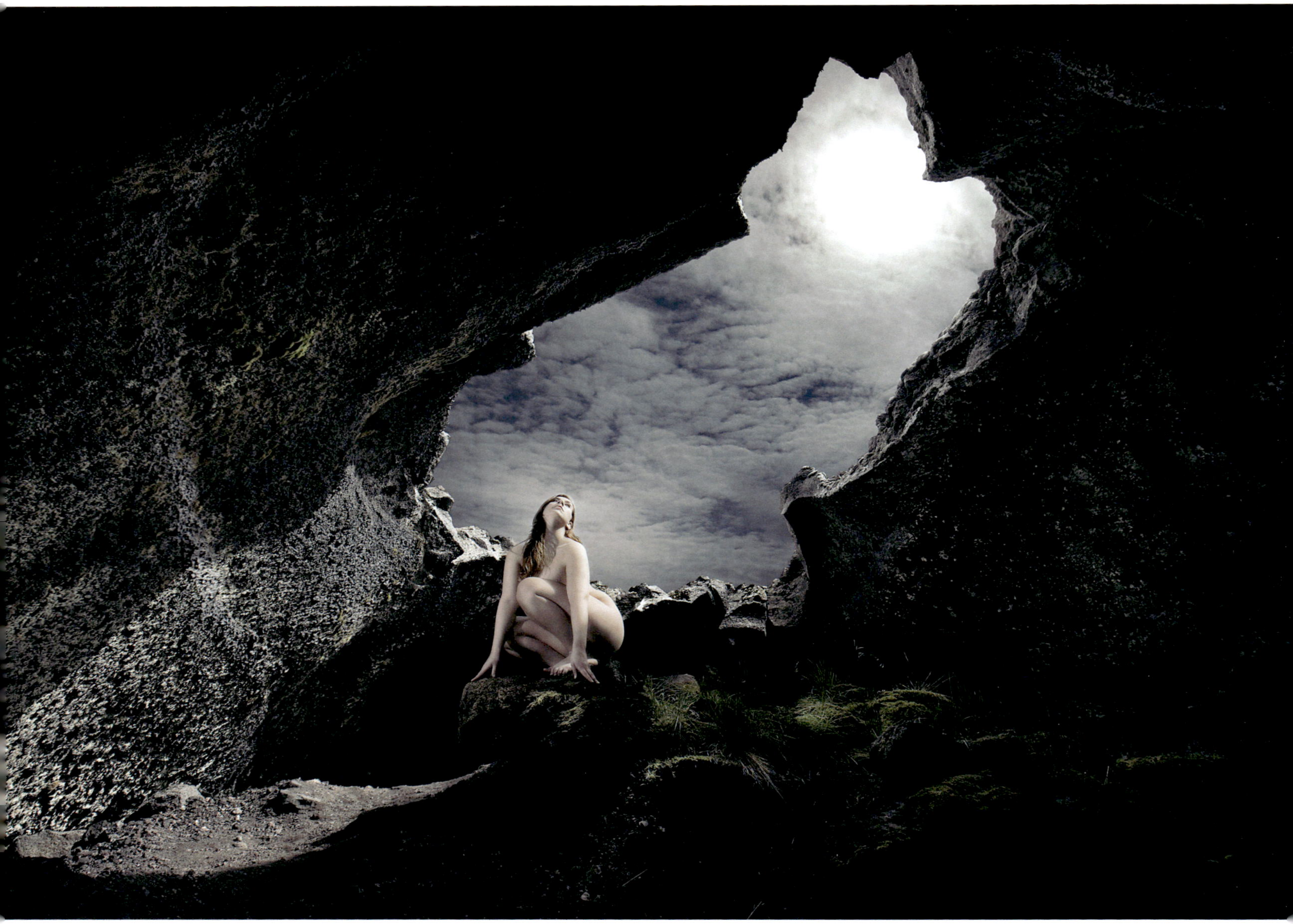

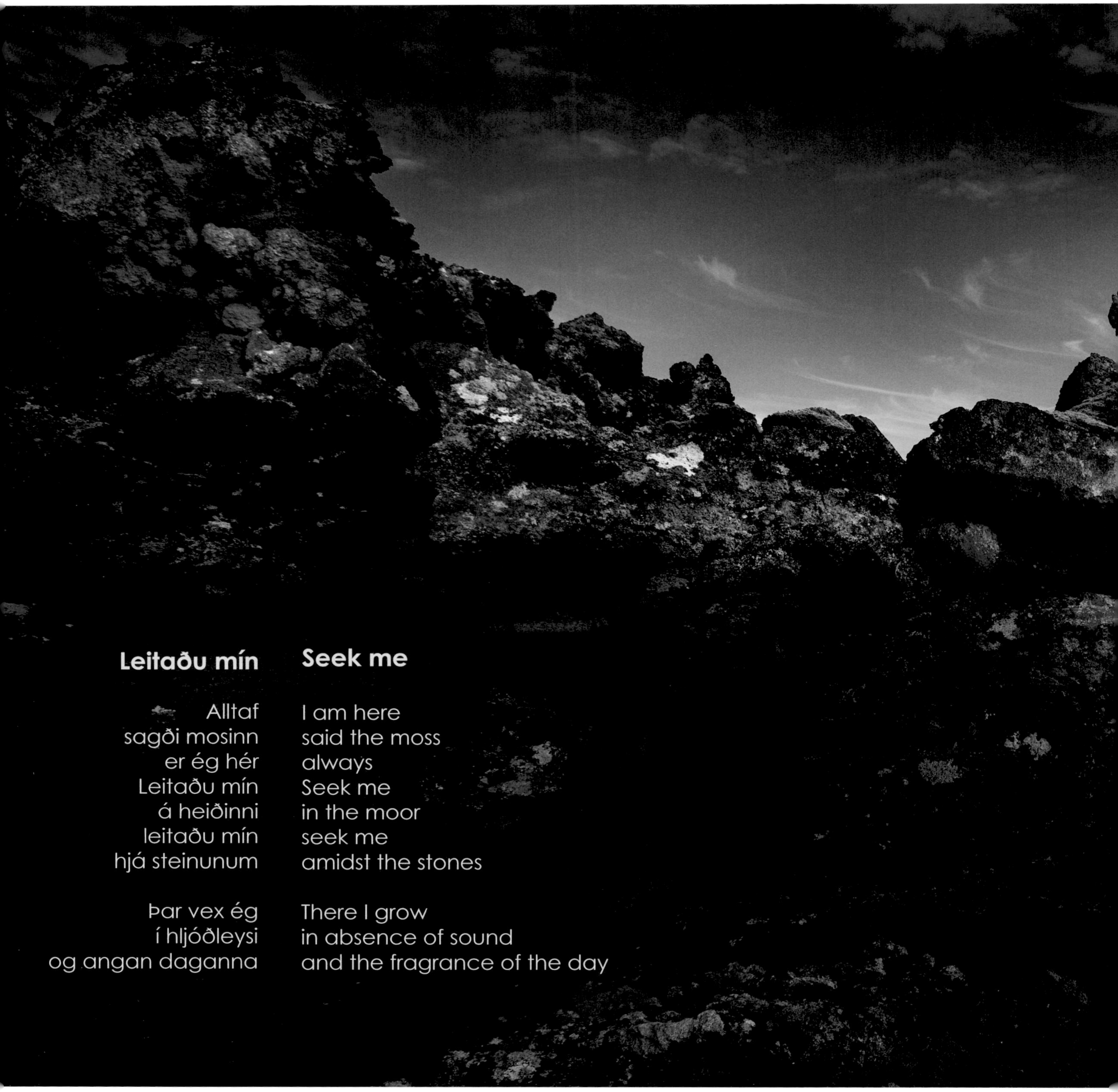

Leitaðu mín

Alltaf
sagði mosinn
er ég hér
Leitaðu mín
á heiðinni
leitaðu mín
hjá steinunum

Þar vex ég
í hljóðleysi
og angan daganna

Seek me

I am here
said the moss
always
Seek me
in the moor
seek me
amidst the stones

There I grow
in absence of sound
and the fragrance of the day

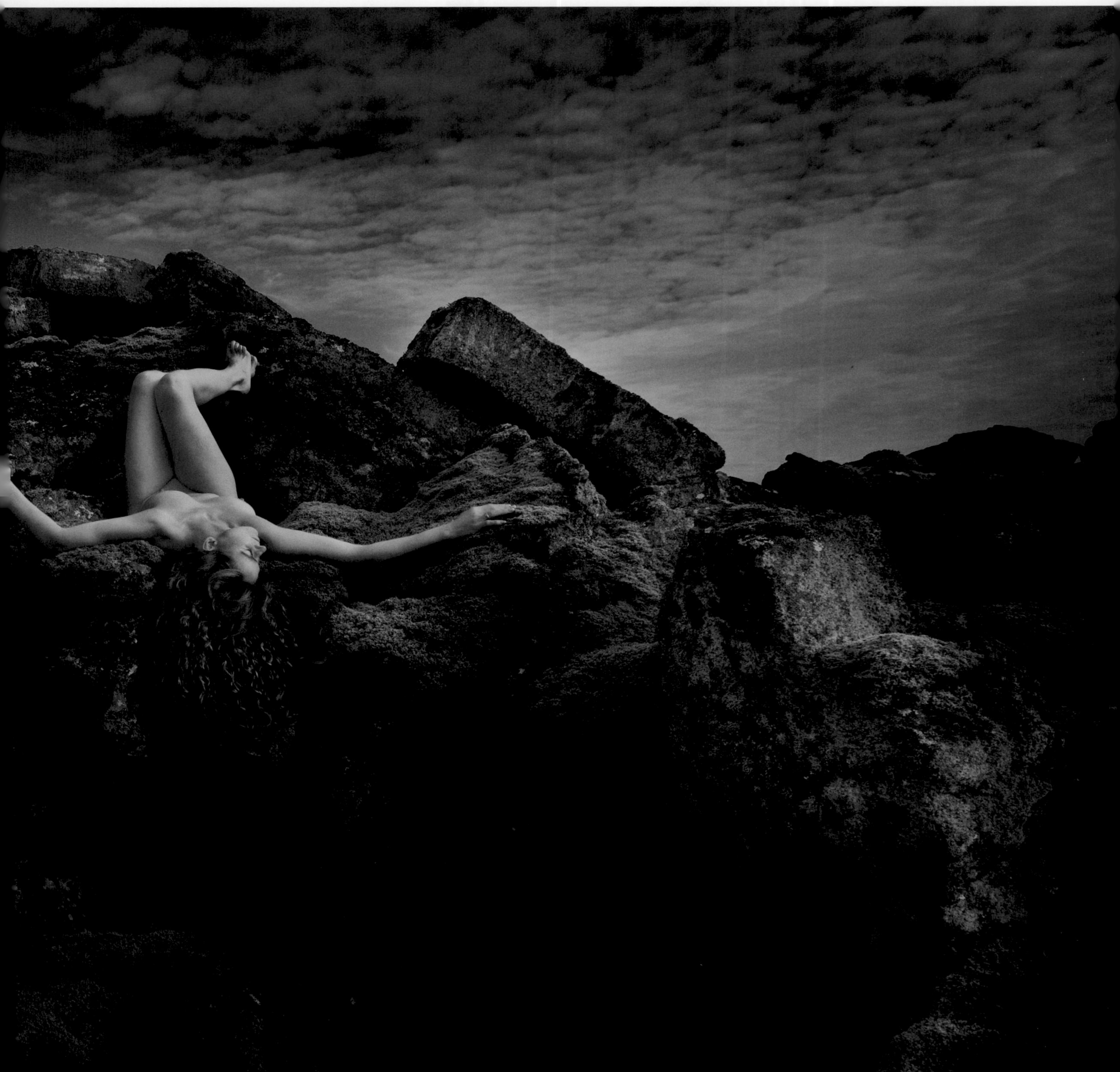

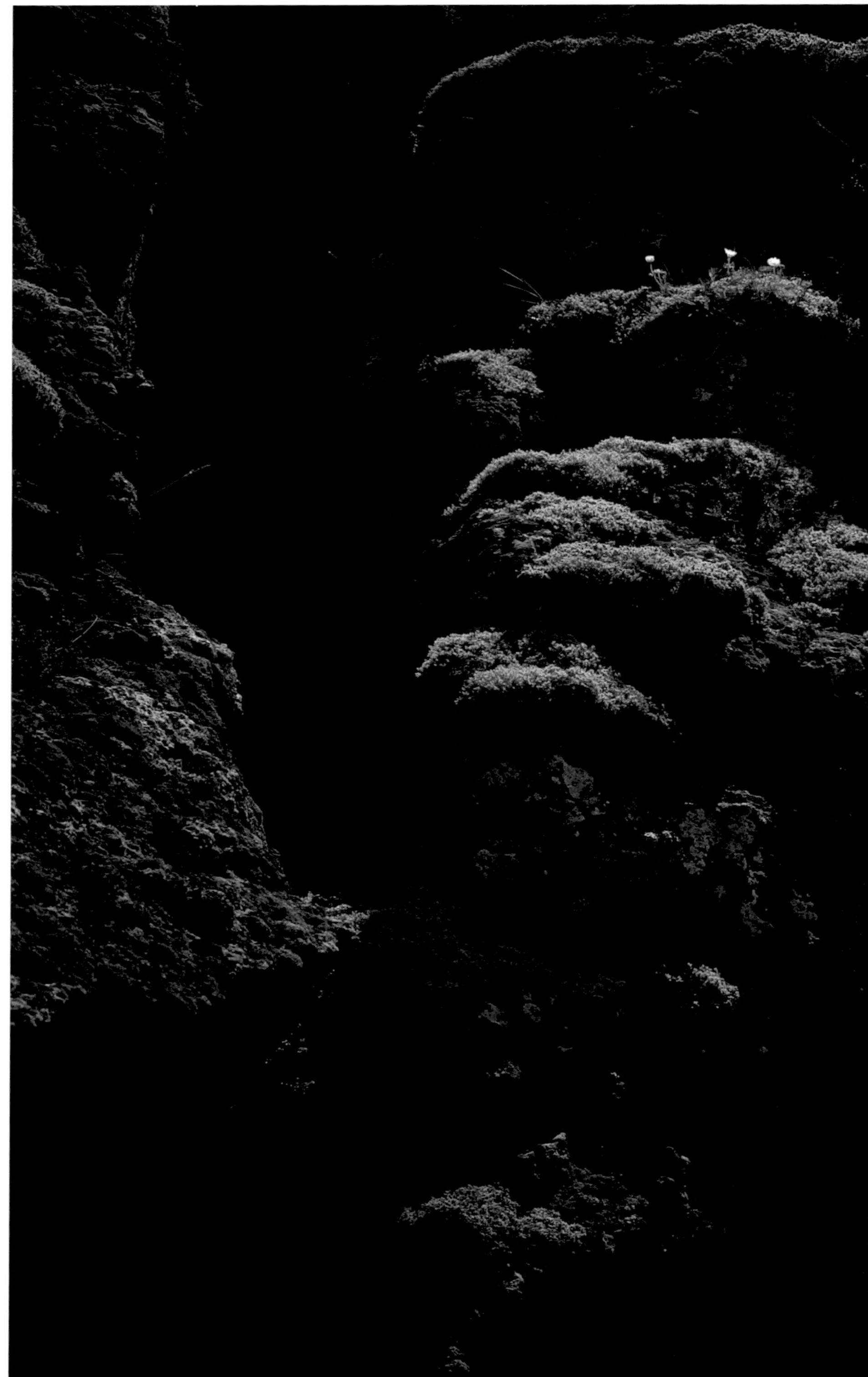

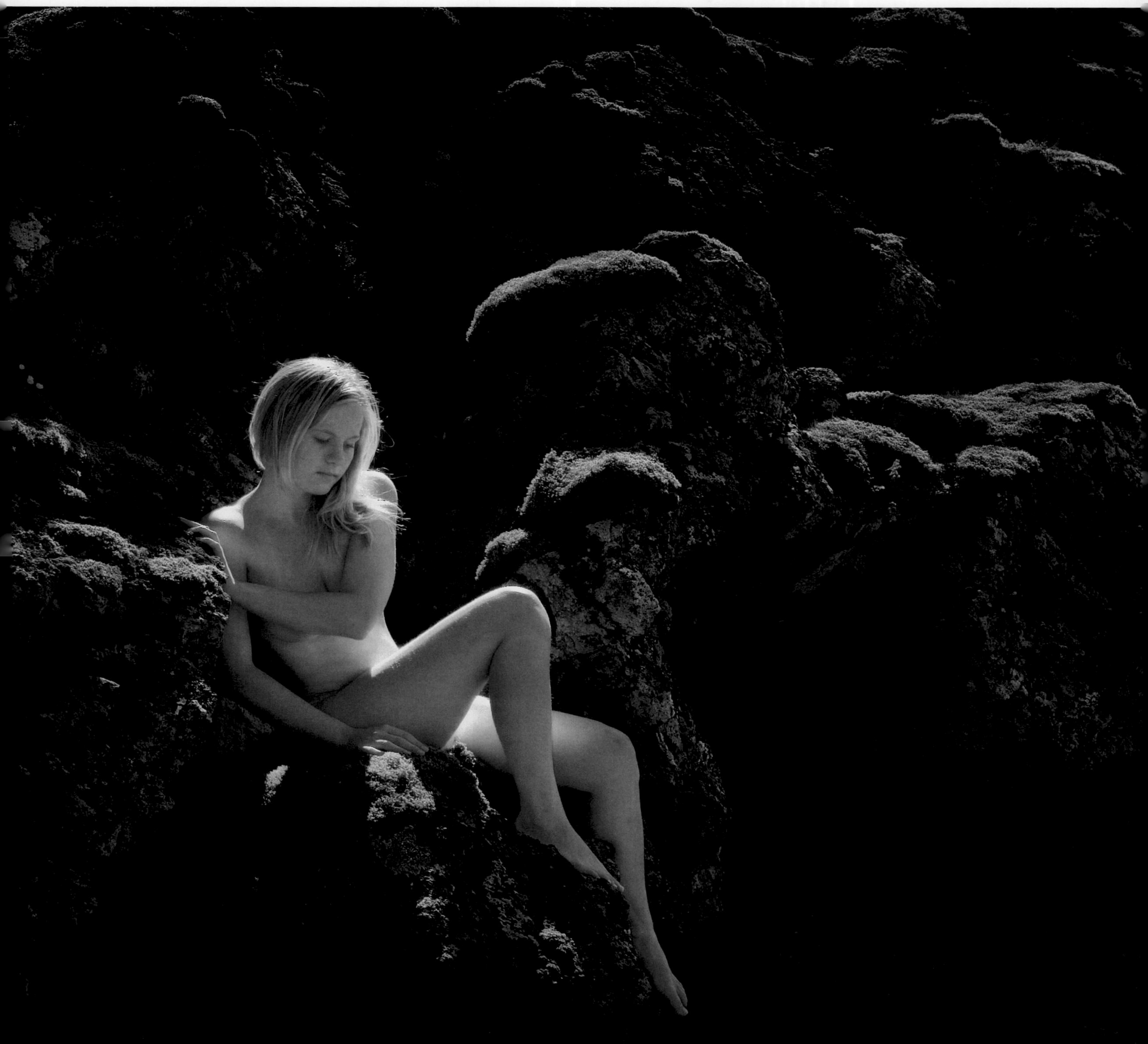

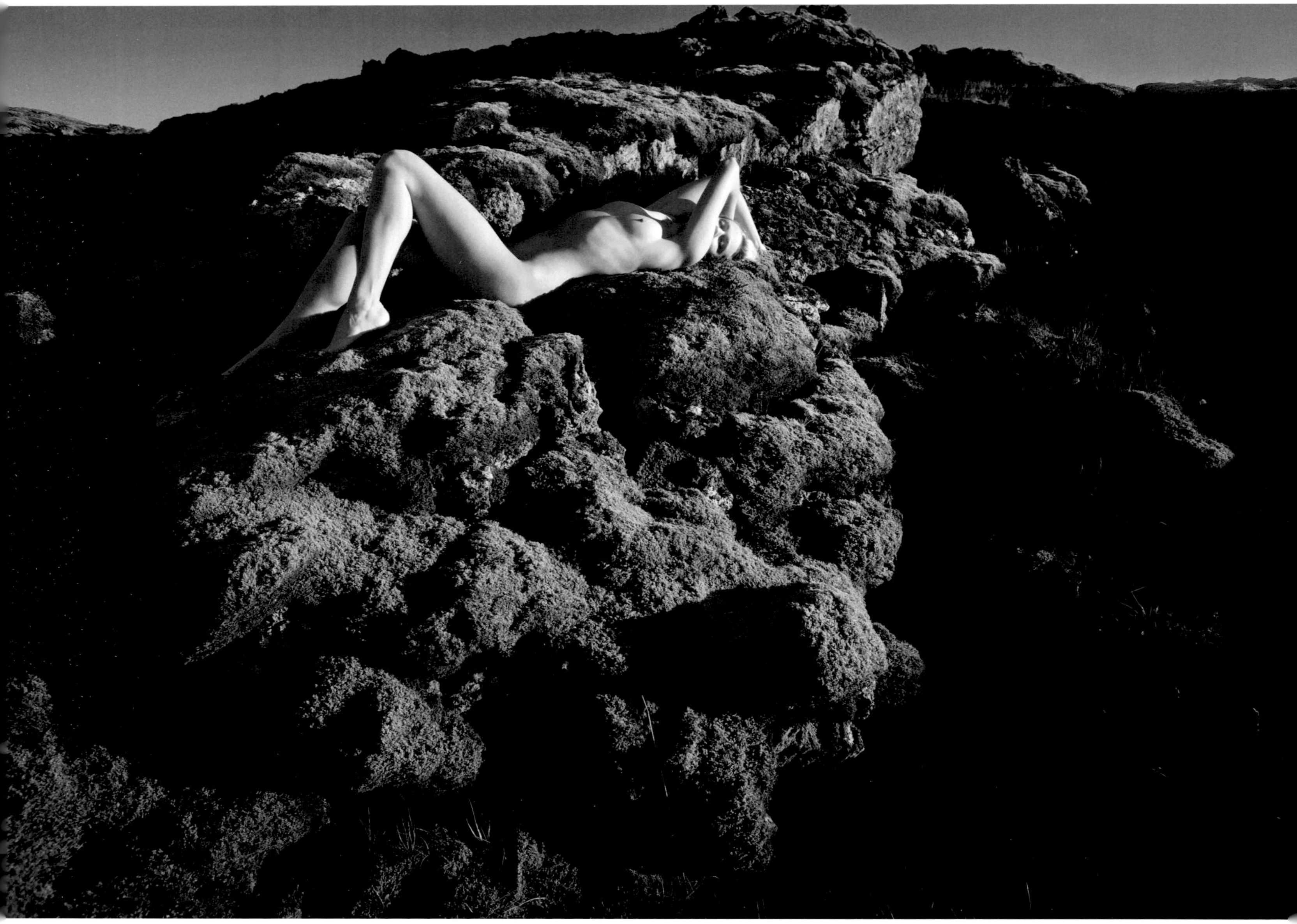

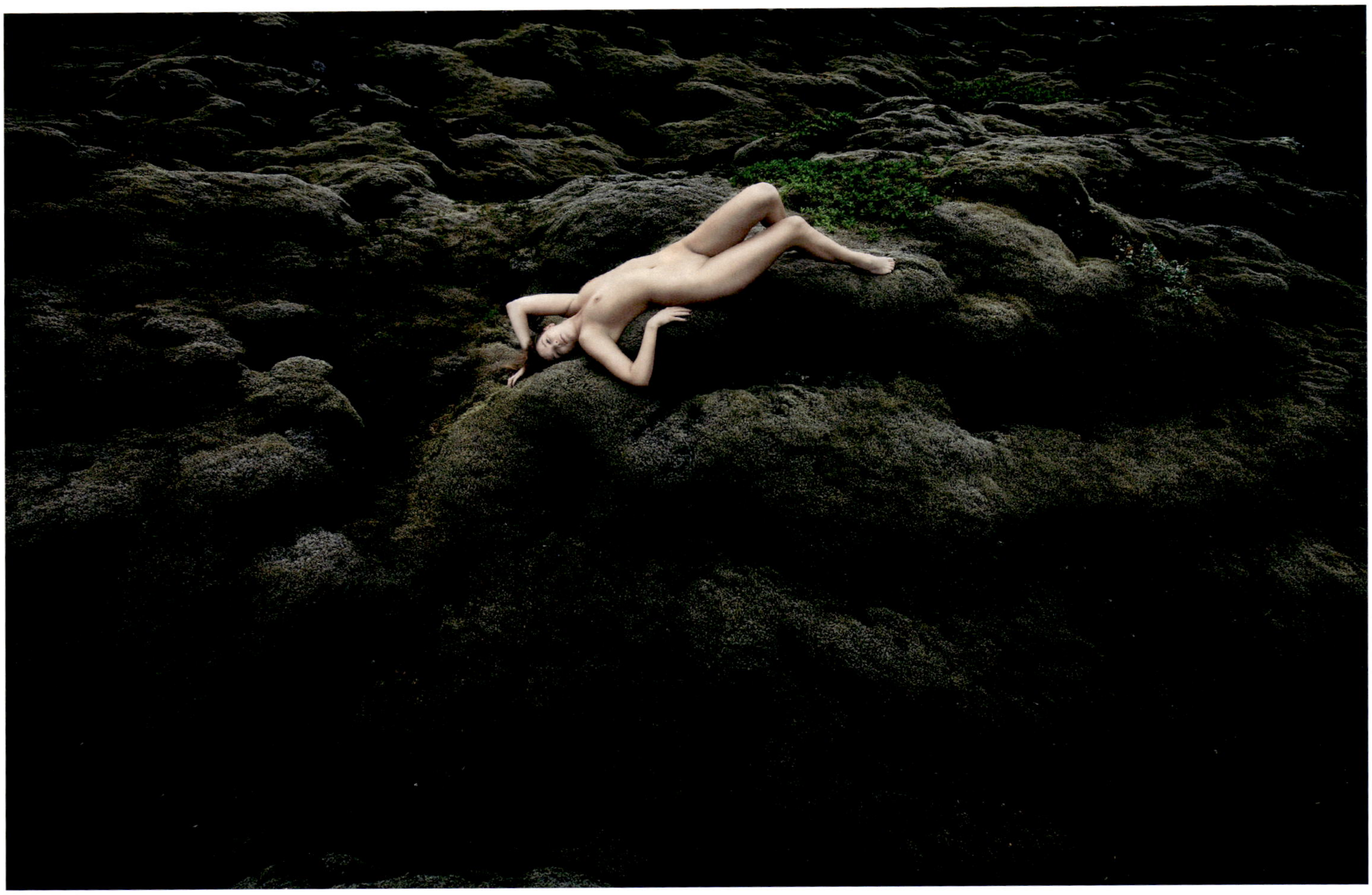

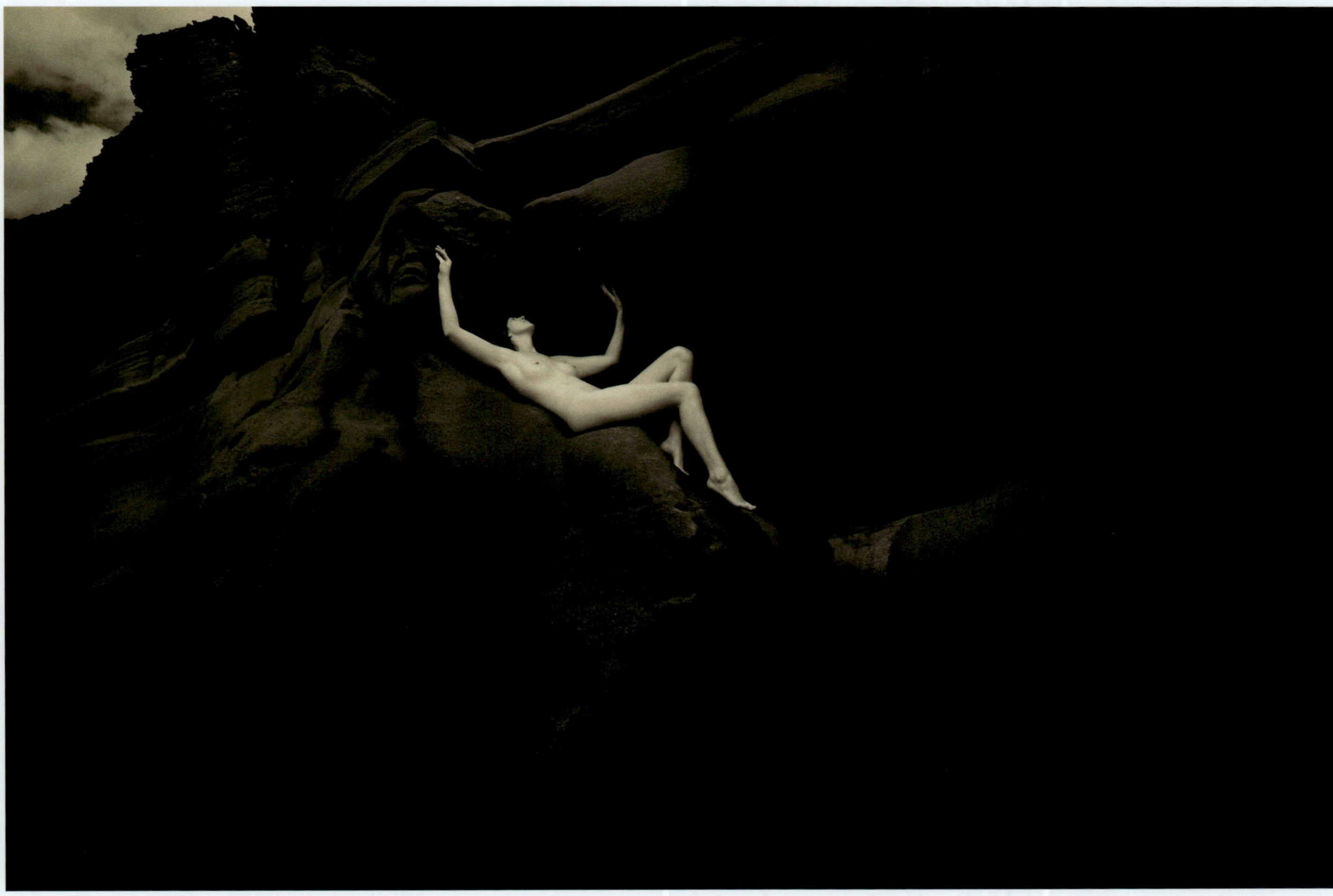

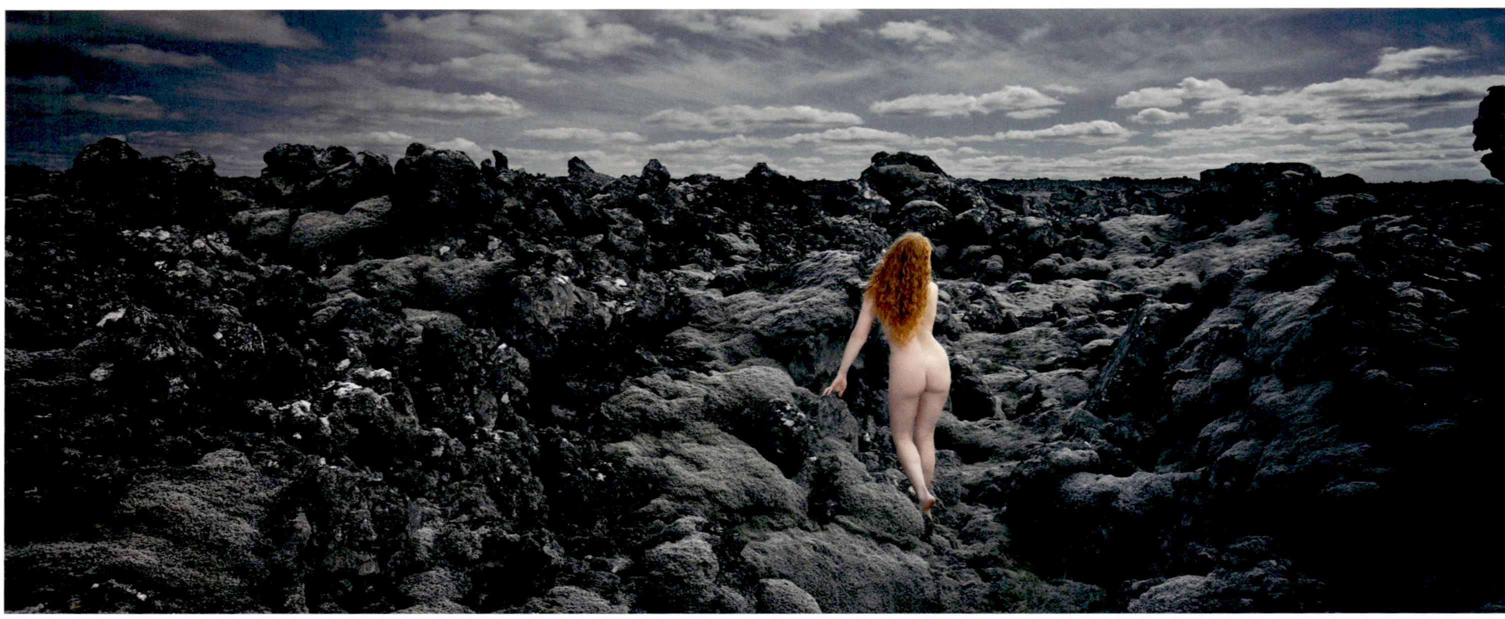

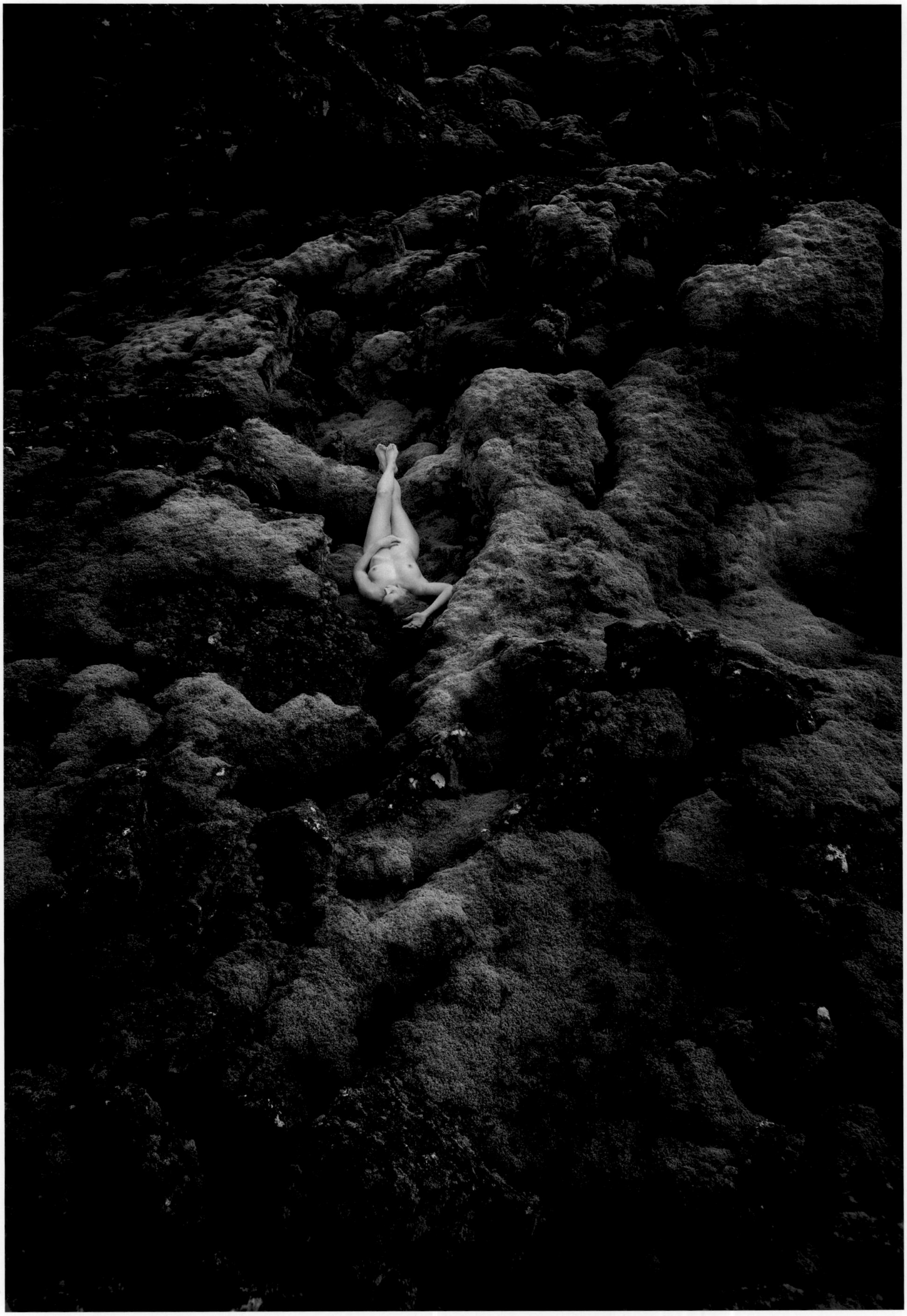

Brennandi sólskin

Að elska
er að játast þjáningu
sem gefur lífinu
lit og skugga

Að elska
er að standa aleinn
í brennandi sólskini
langa að flýja
en geta sig hvergi hrært

Blazing Sunshine

Loving
is accepting pain
which gives life
colors and shadows

Loving
is standing alone
in blazing sunshine
wanting to flee
but unable to move

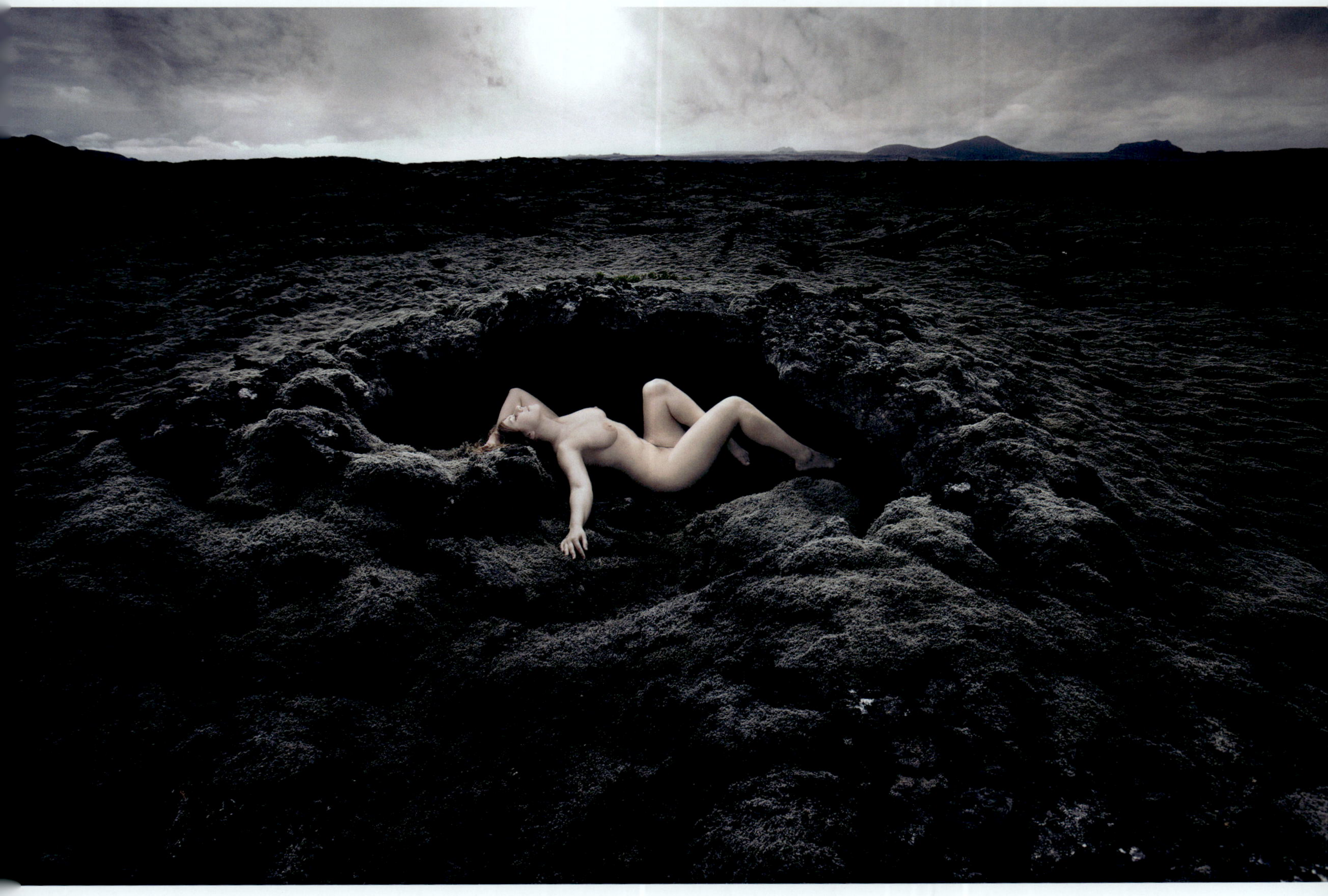

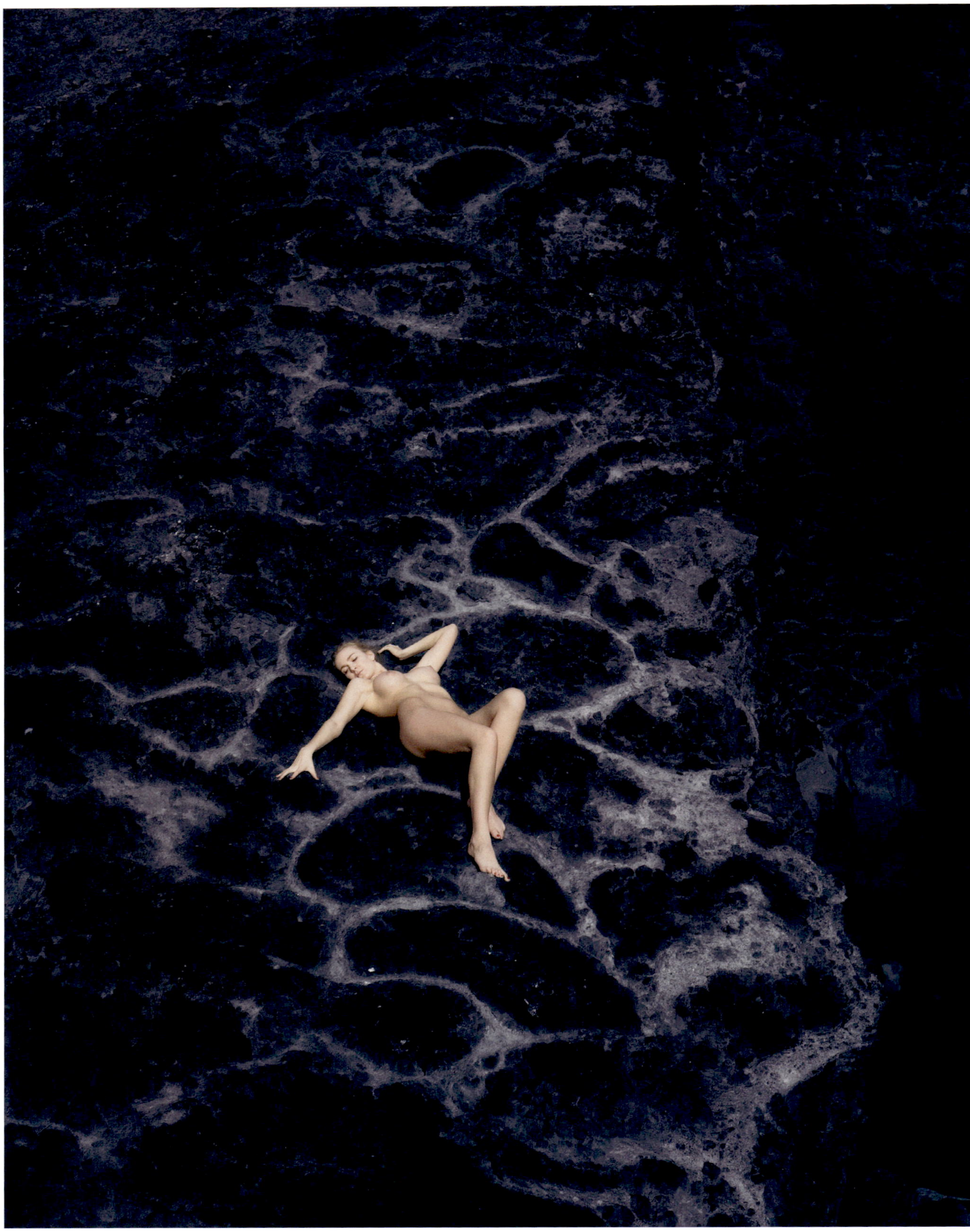

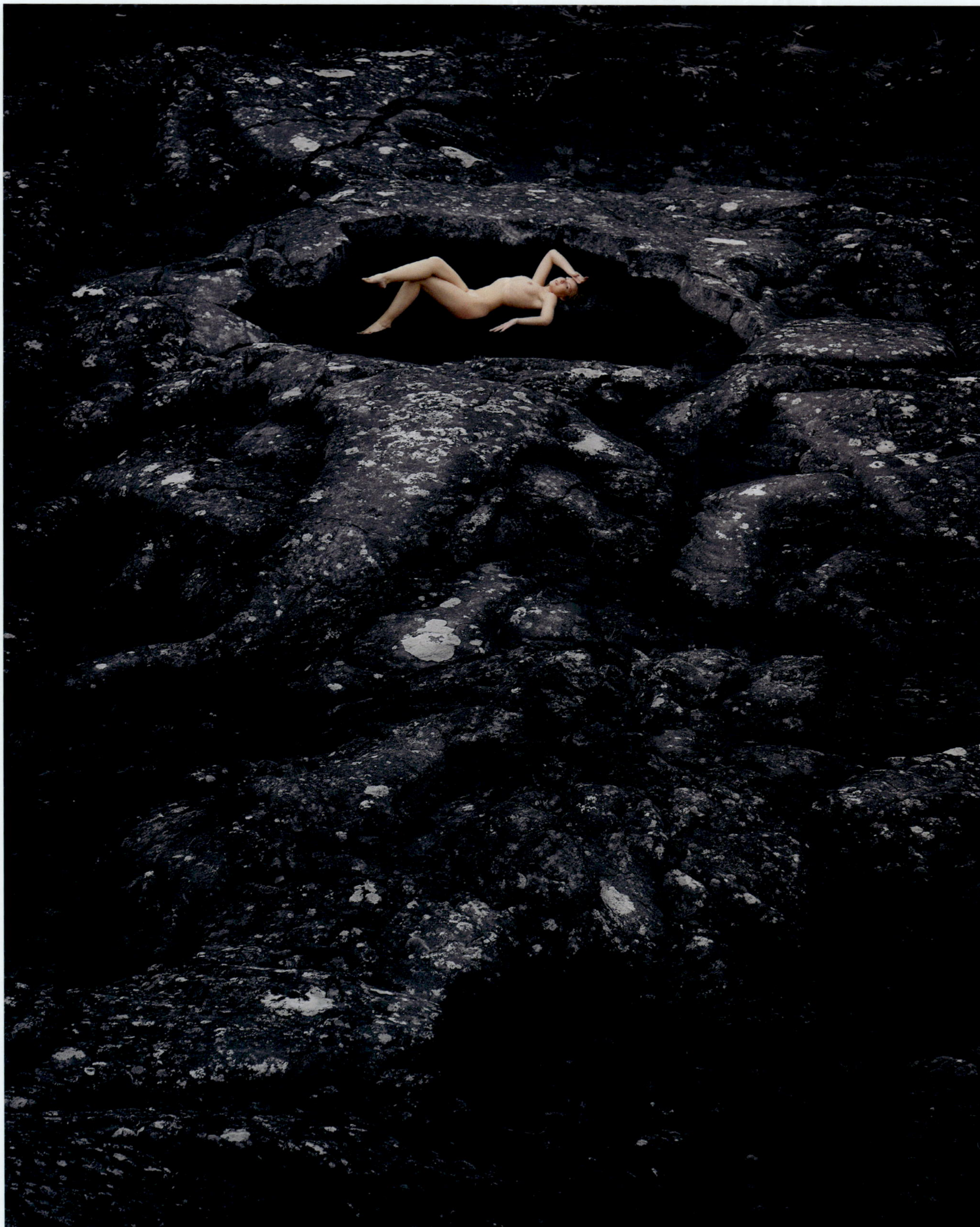

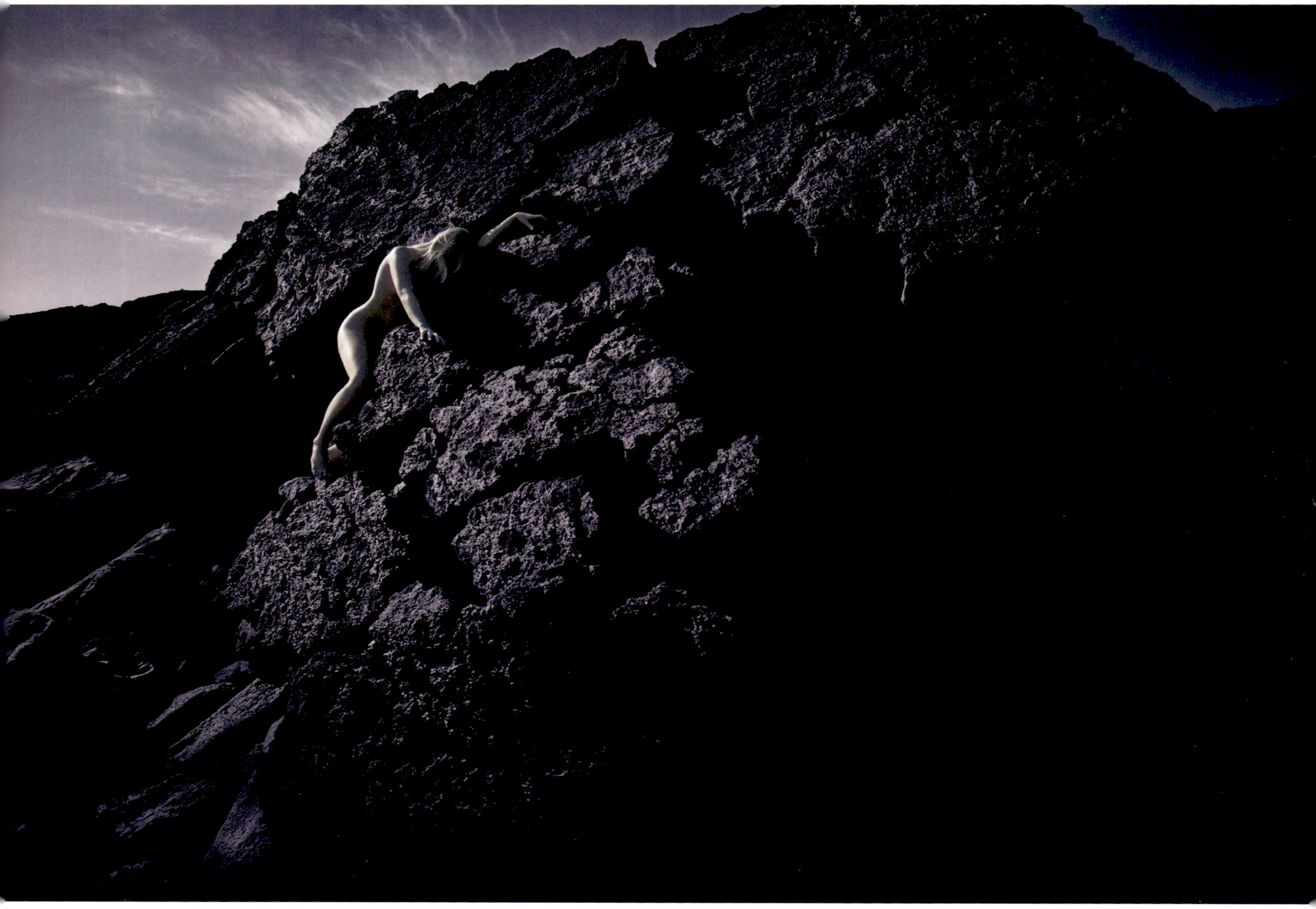

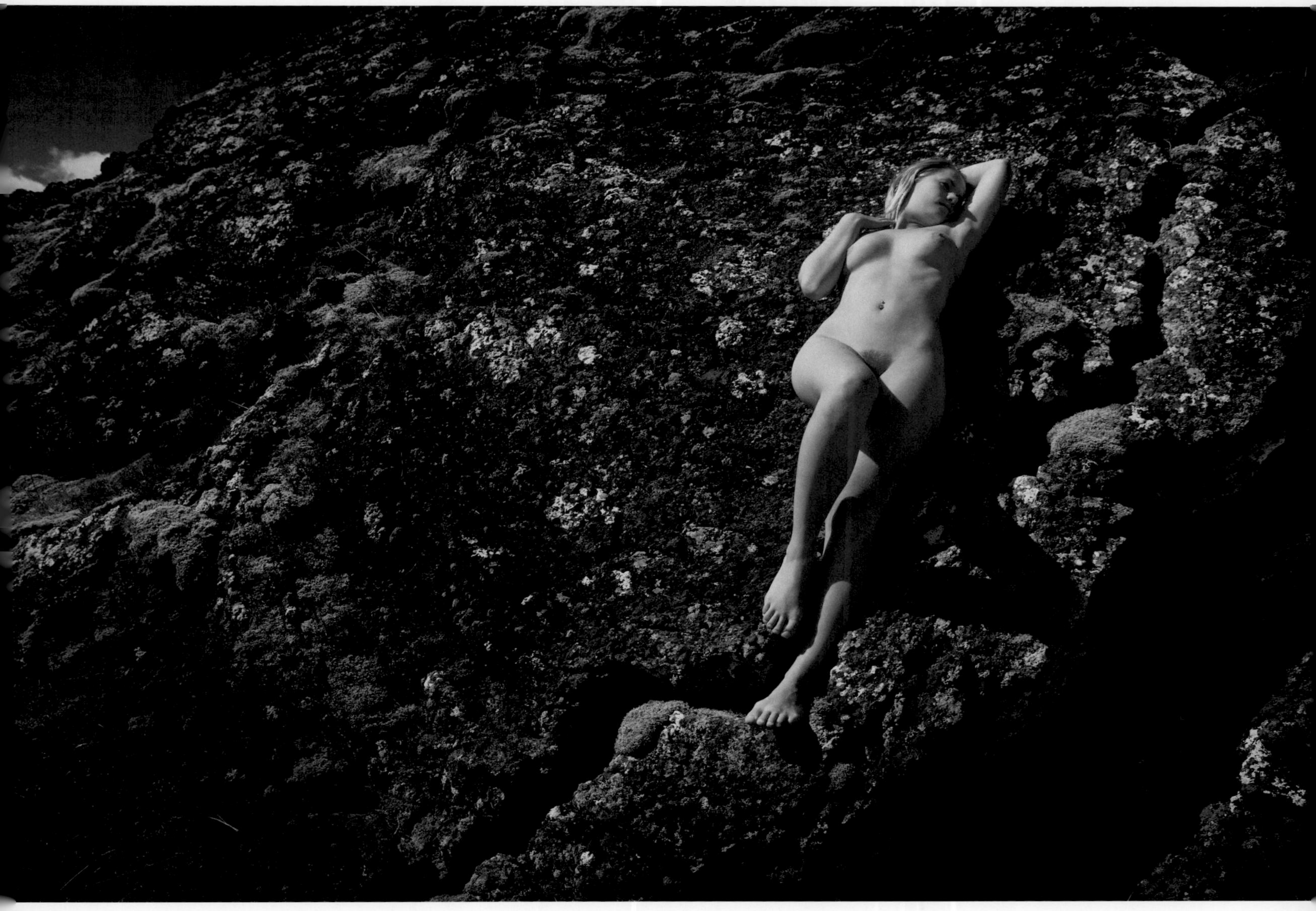

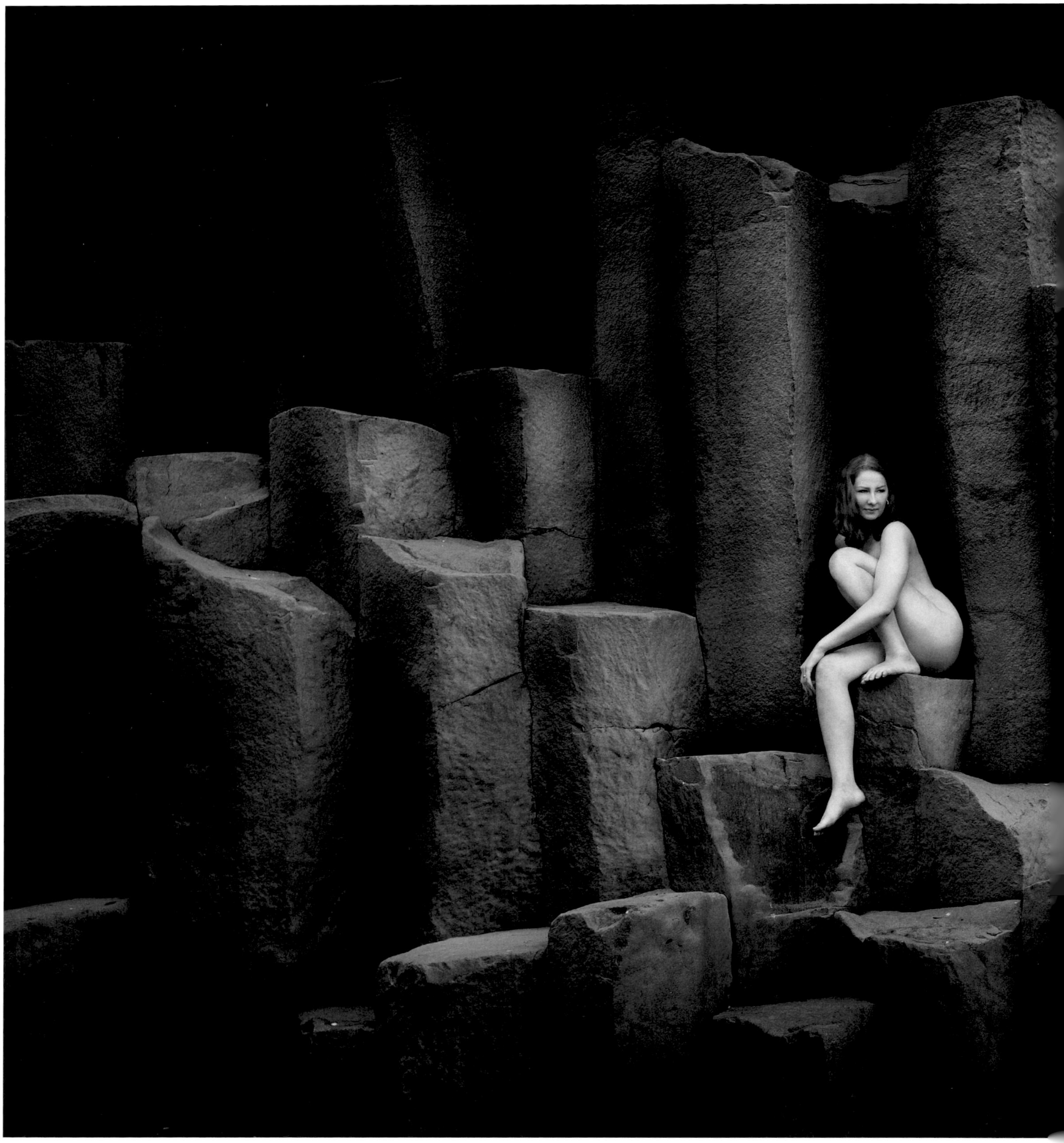

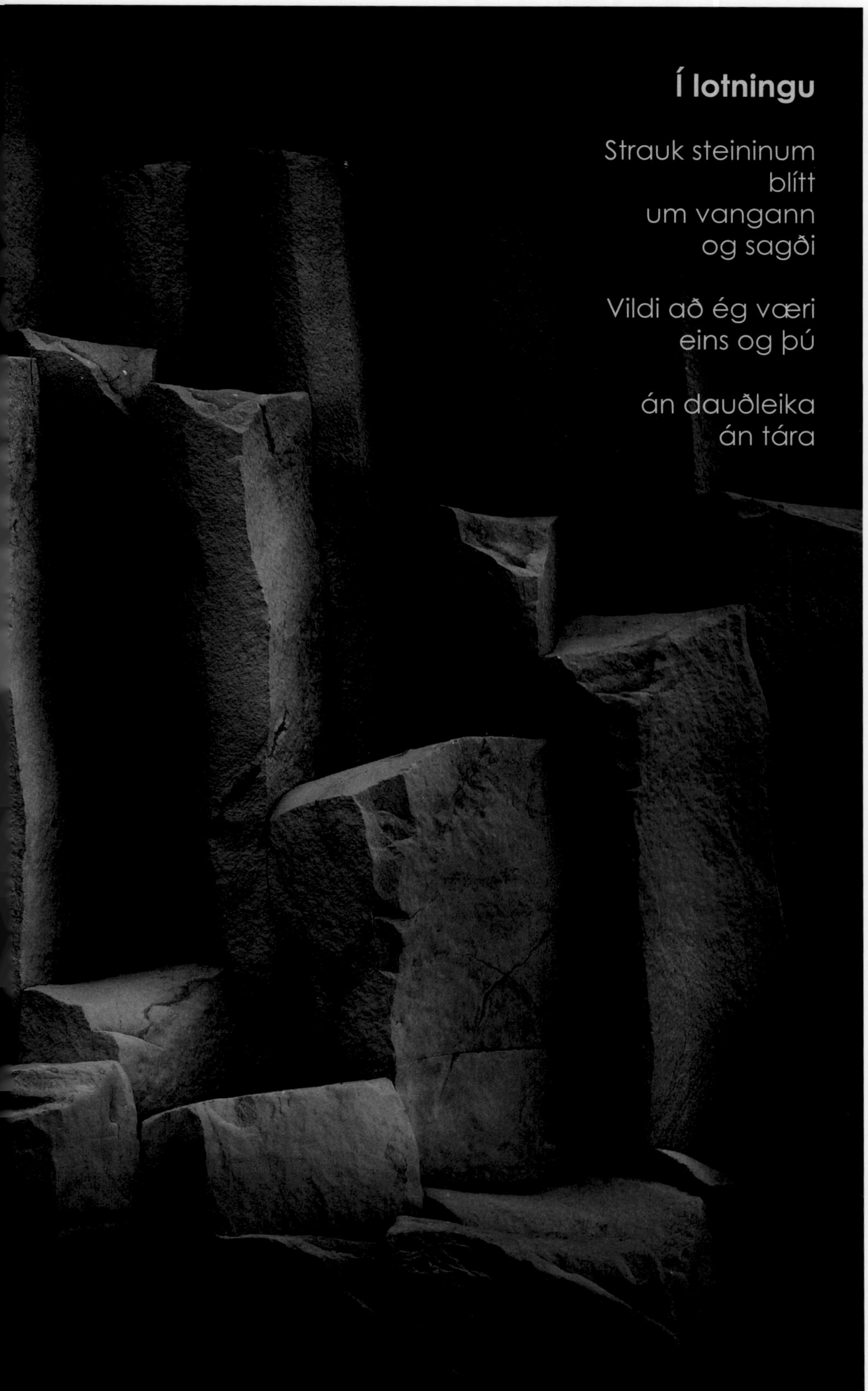

Í lotningu

Strauk steininum
blítt
um vangann
og sagði

Vildi að ég væri
eins og þú

án dauðleika
án tára

In Veneration

Caressed the stone
gently
on the cheek
and said

Wish I were
like you

free of mortality
free from tears

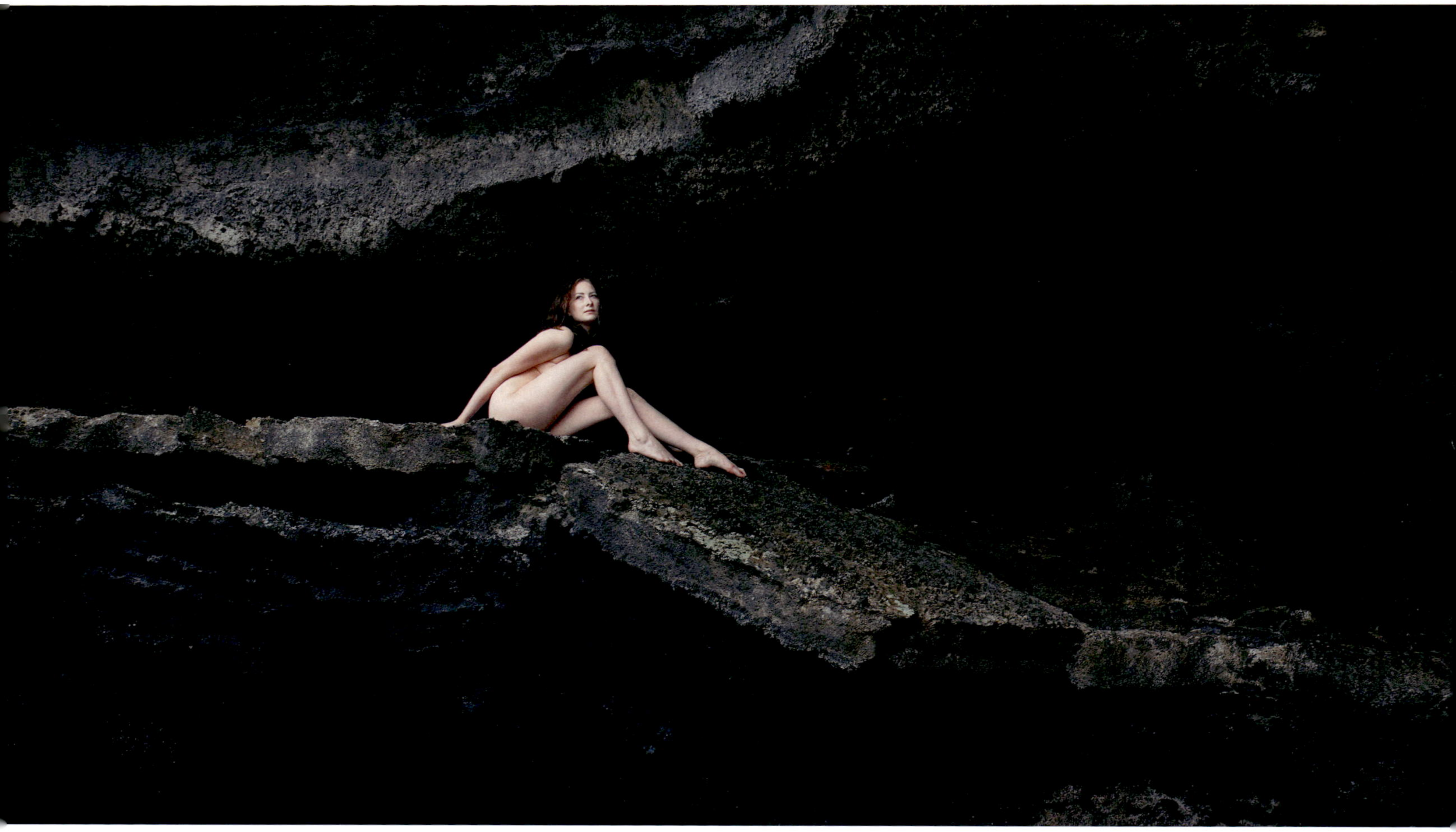

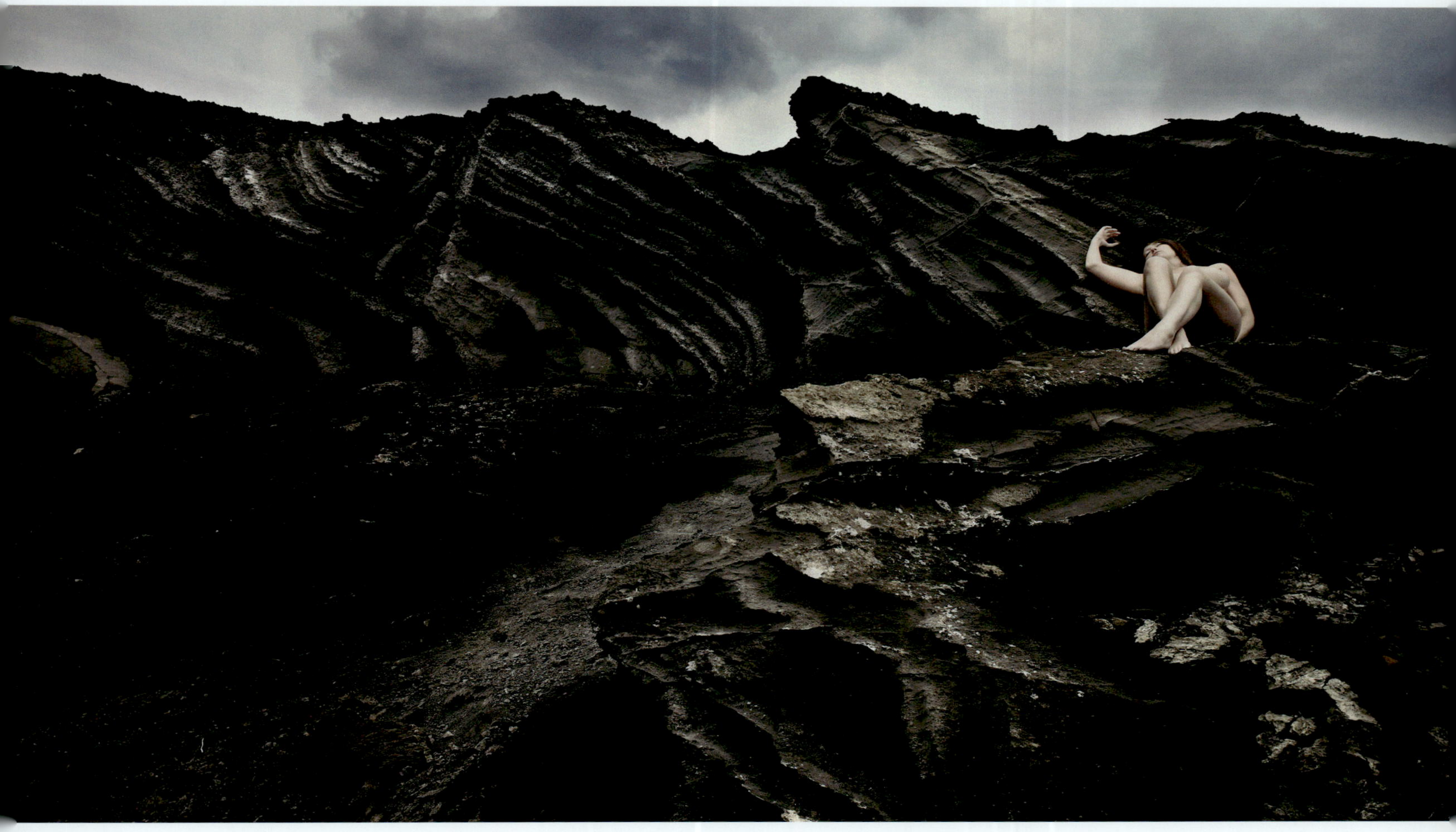

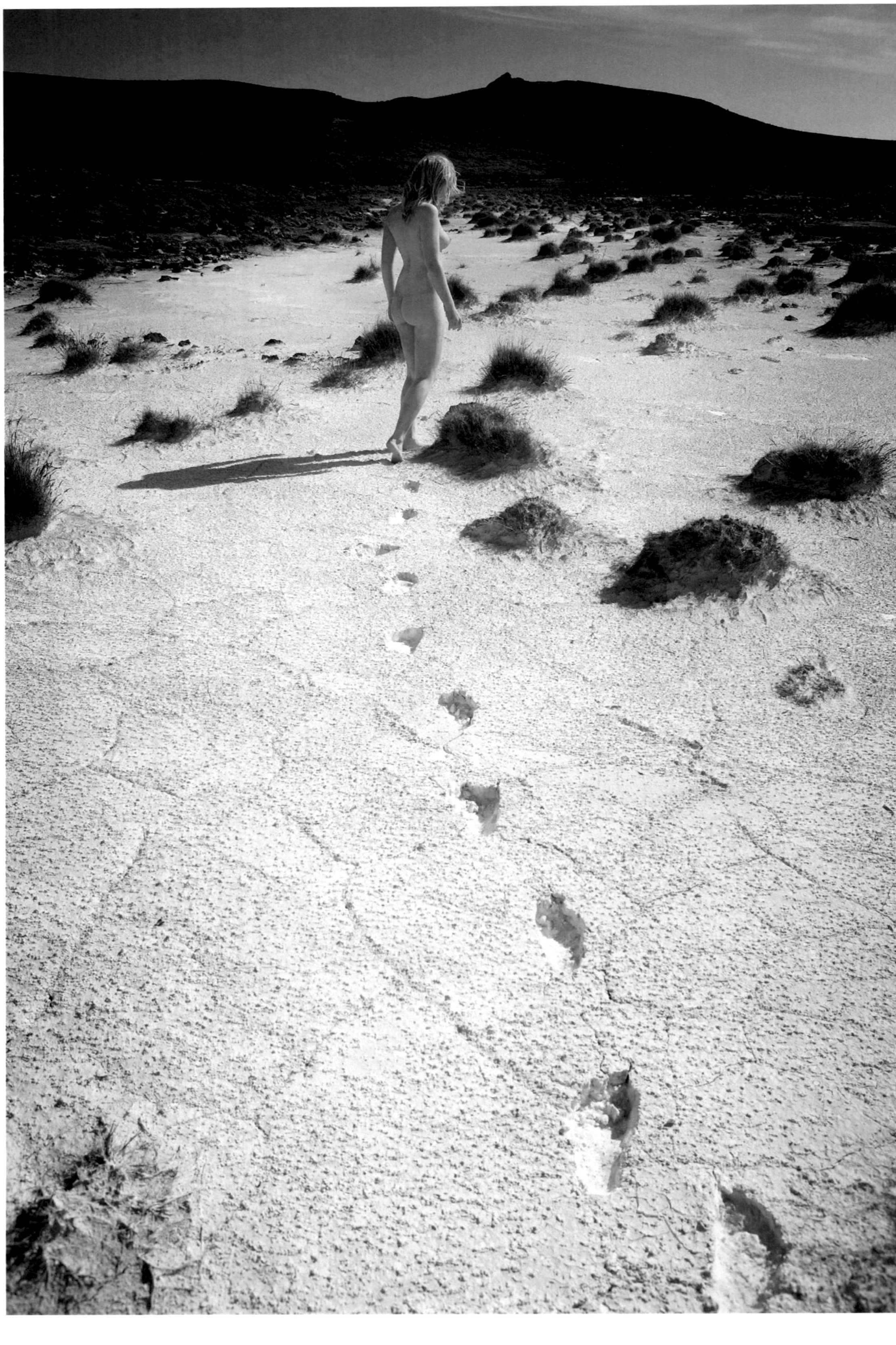

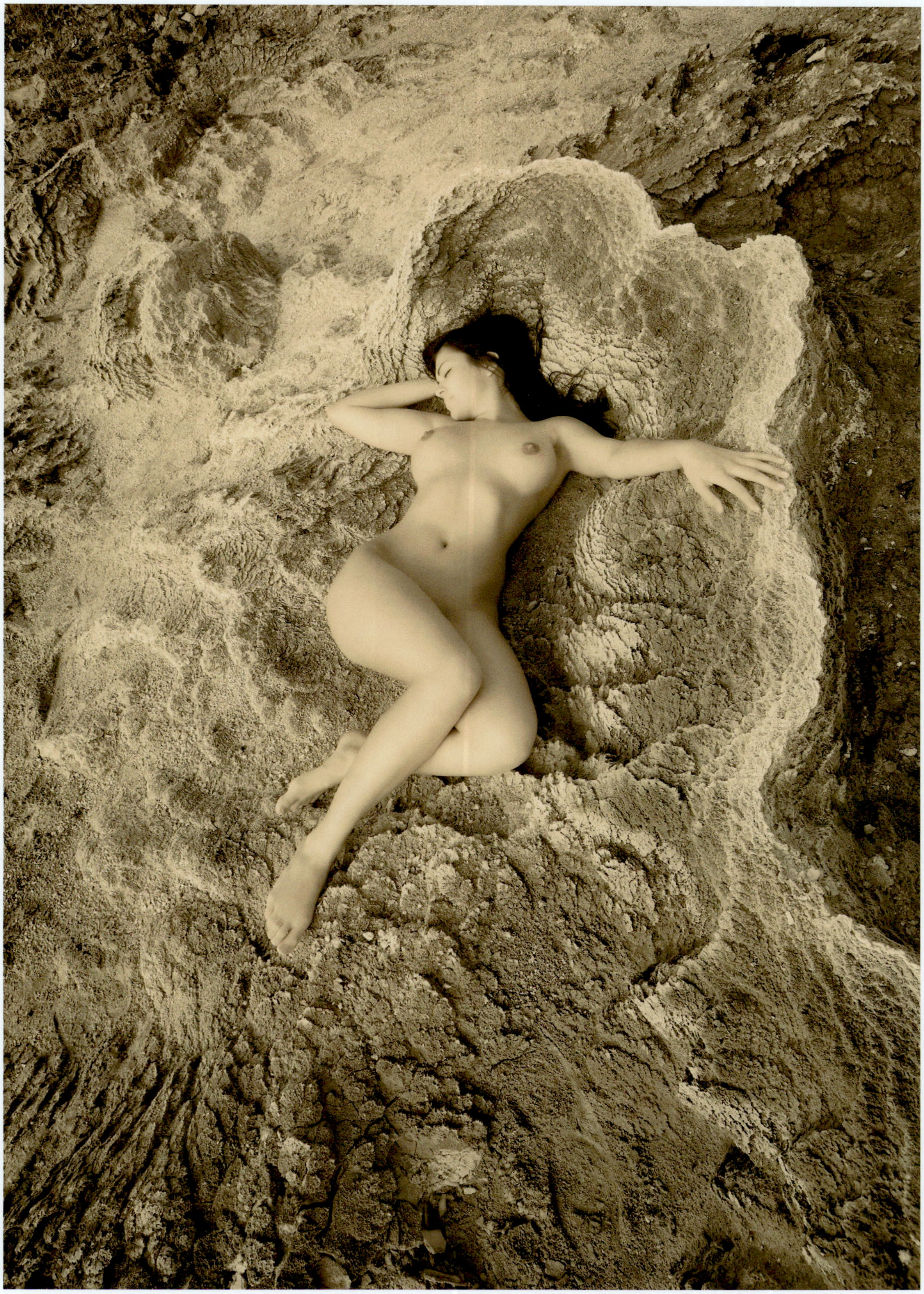

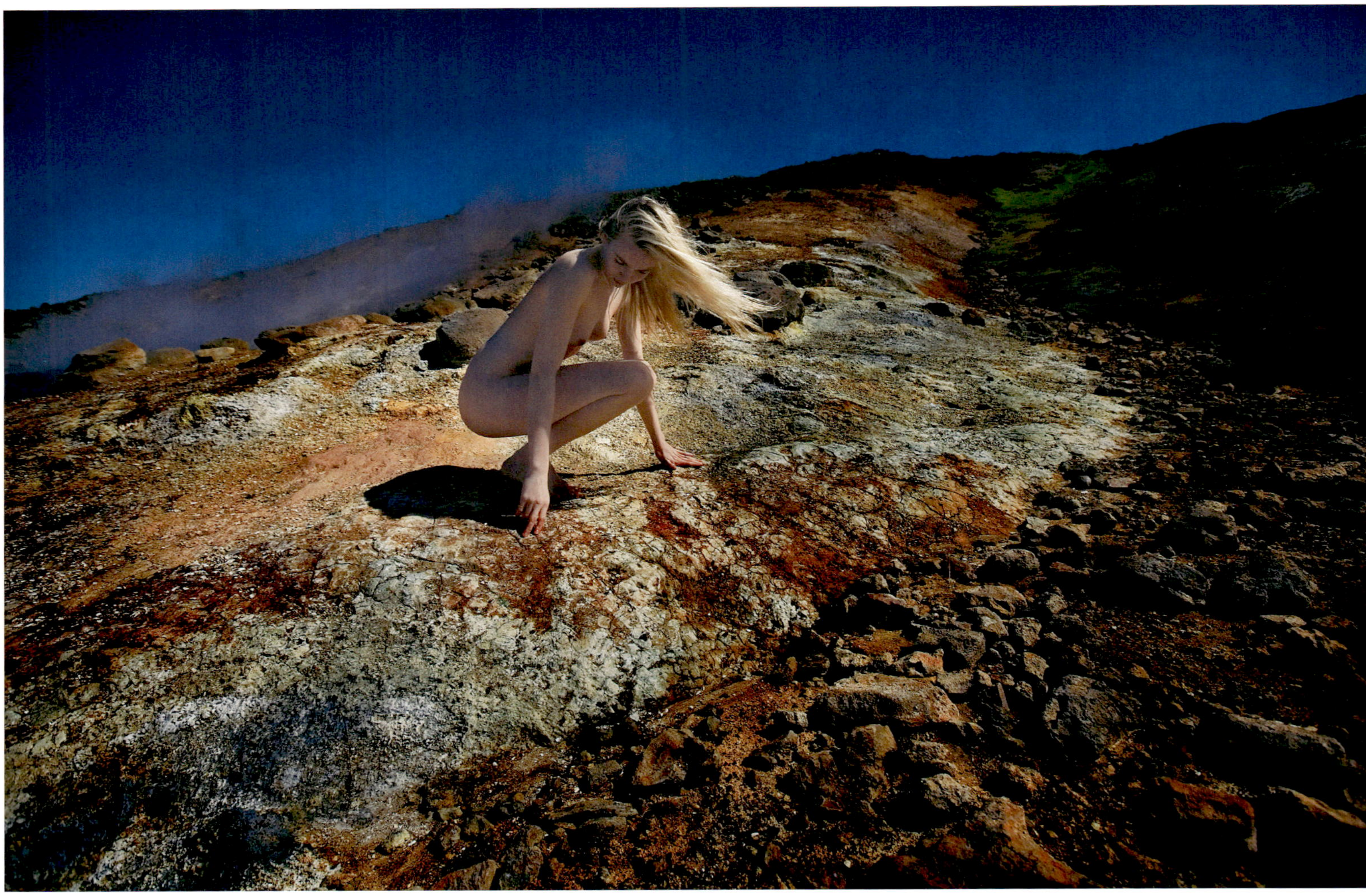

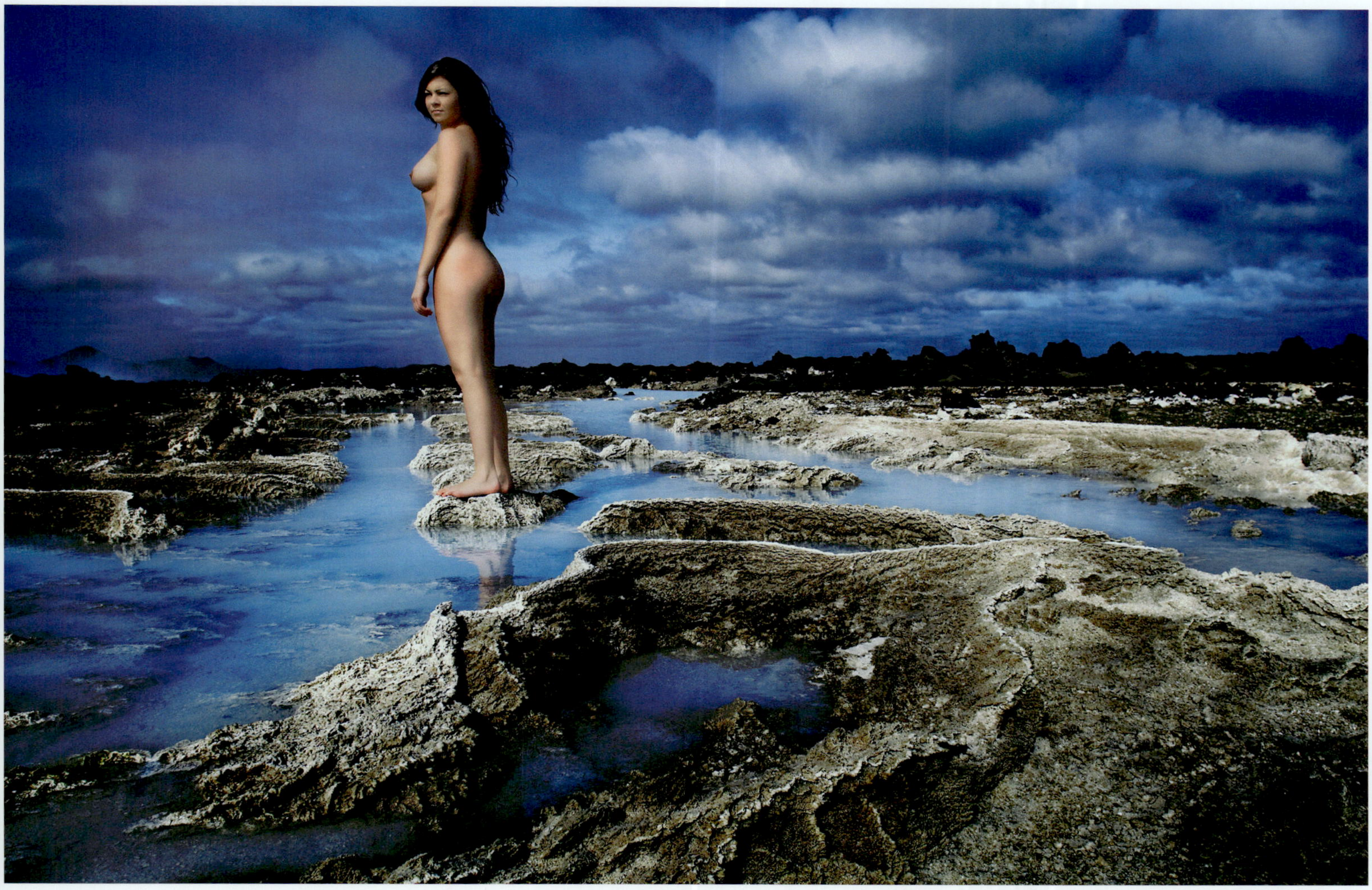

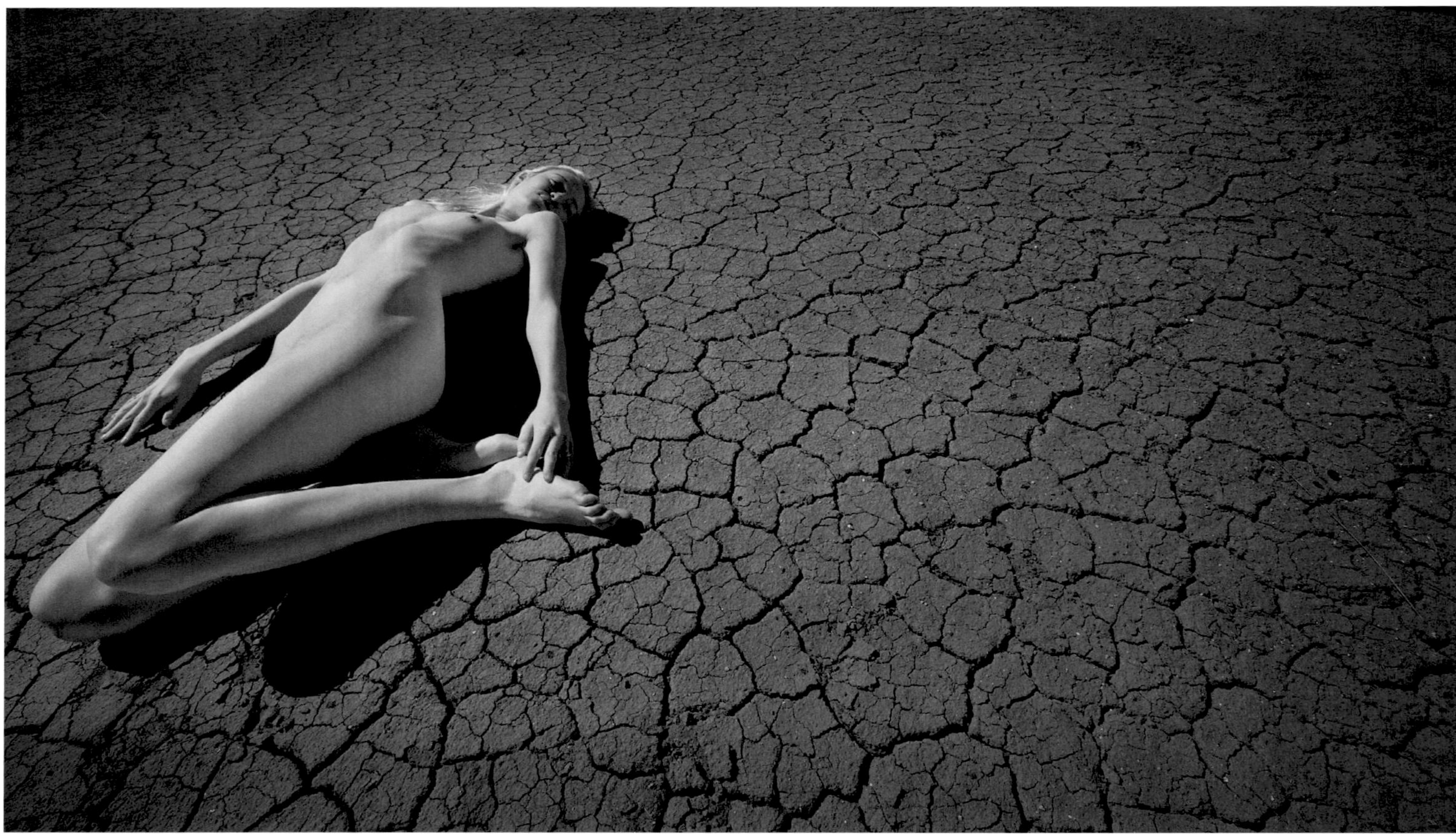

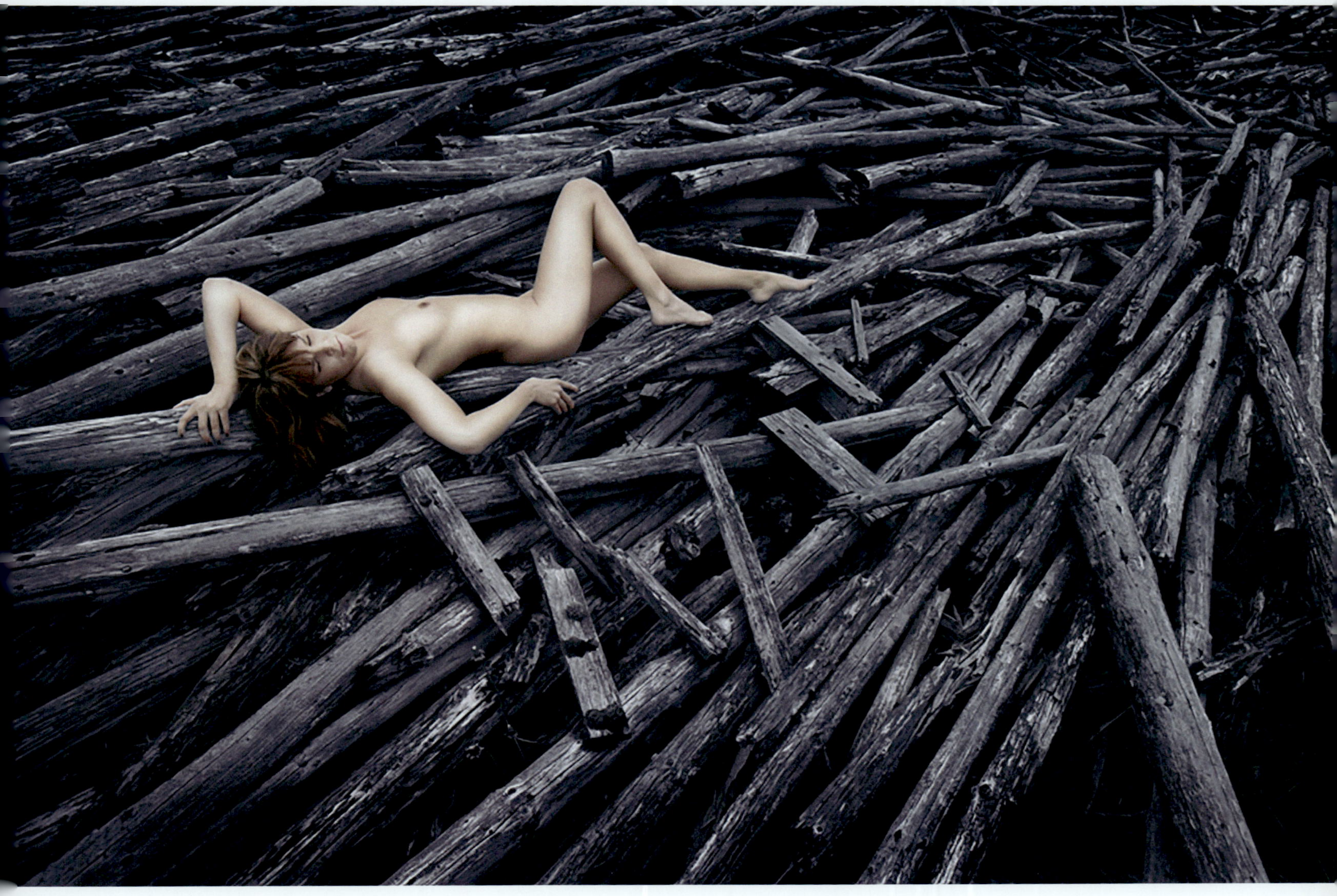

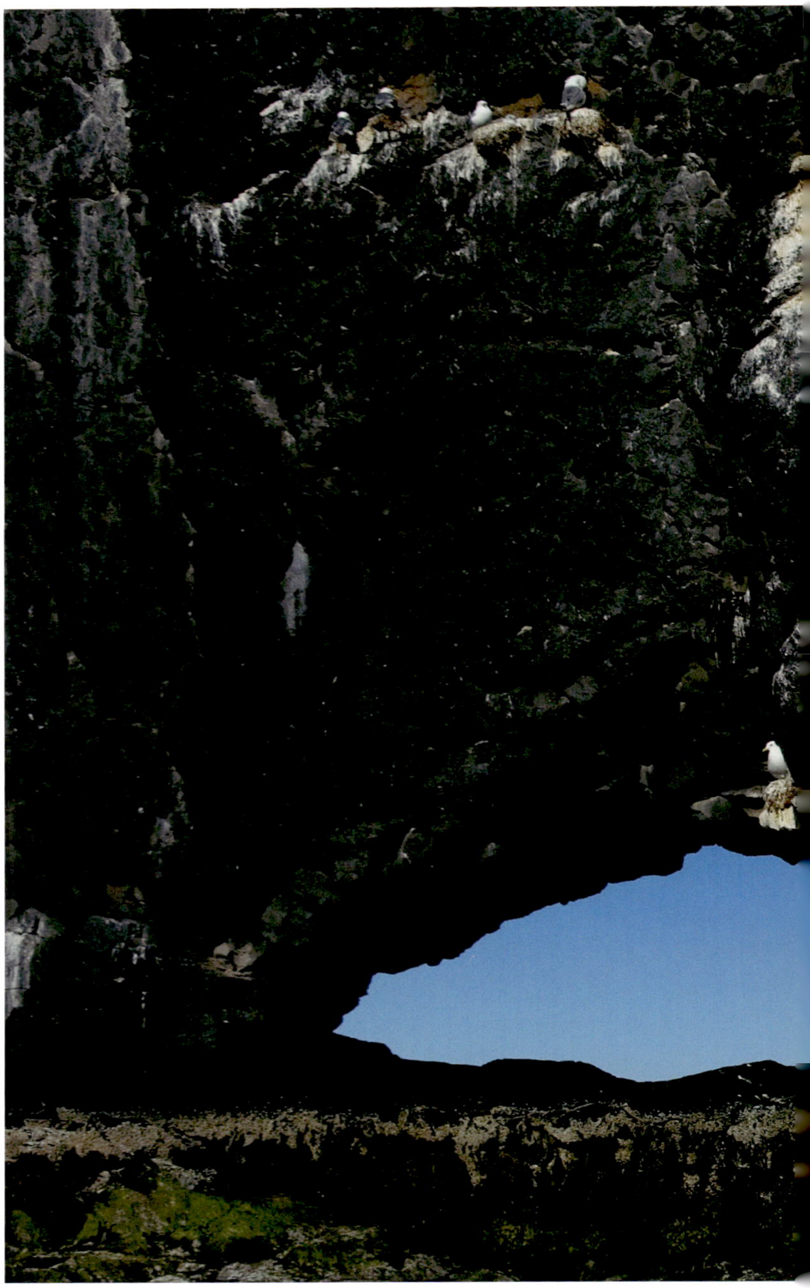

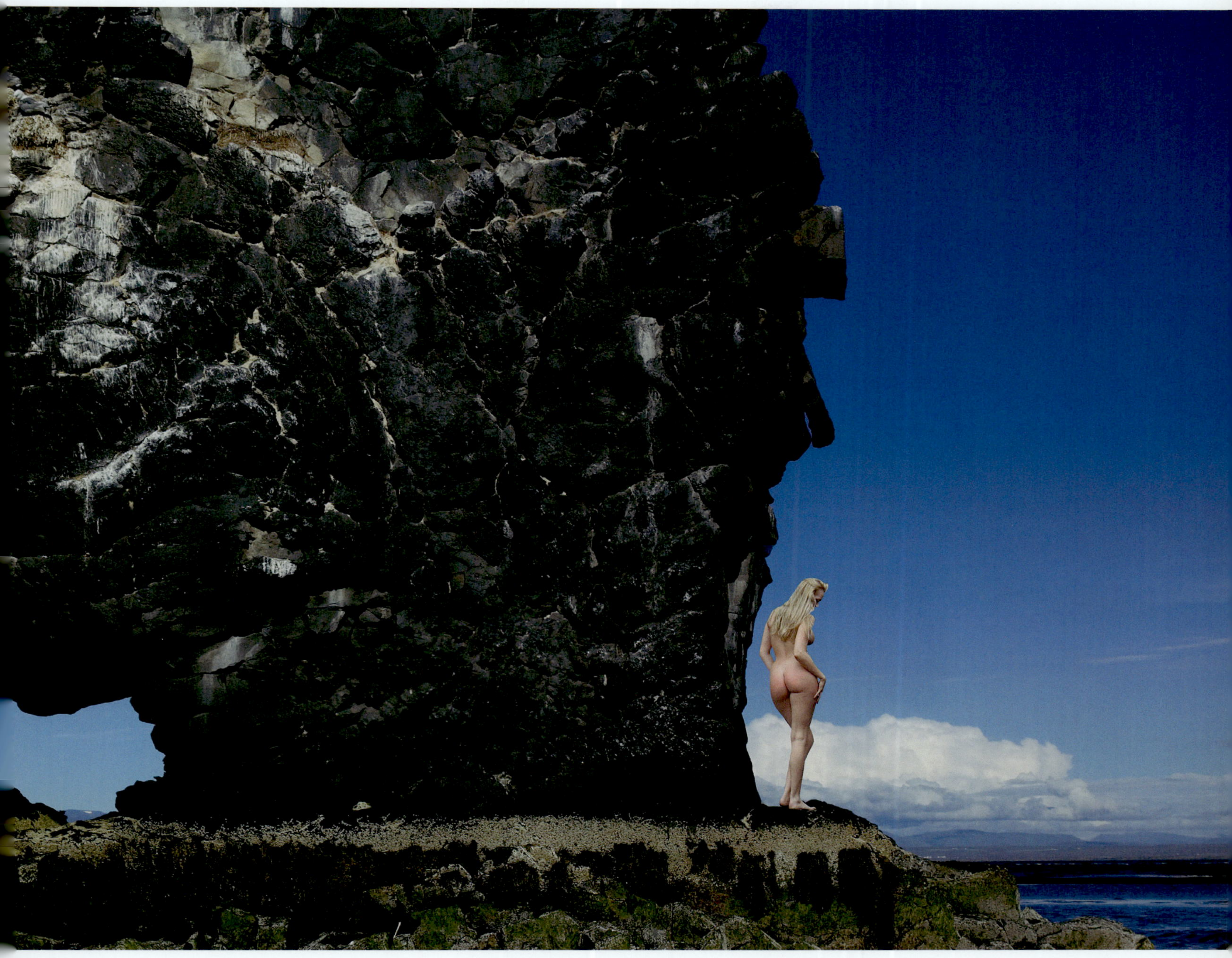

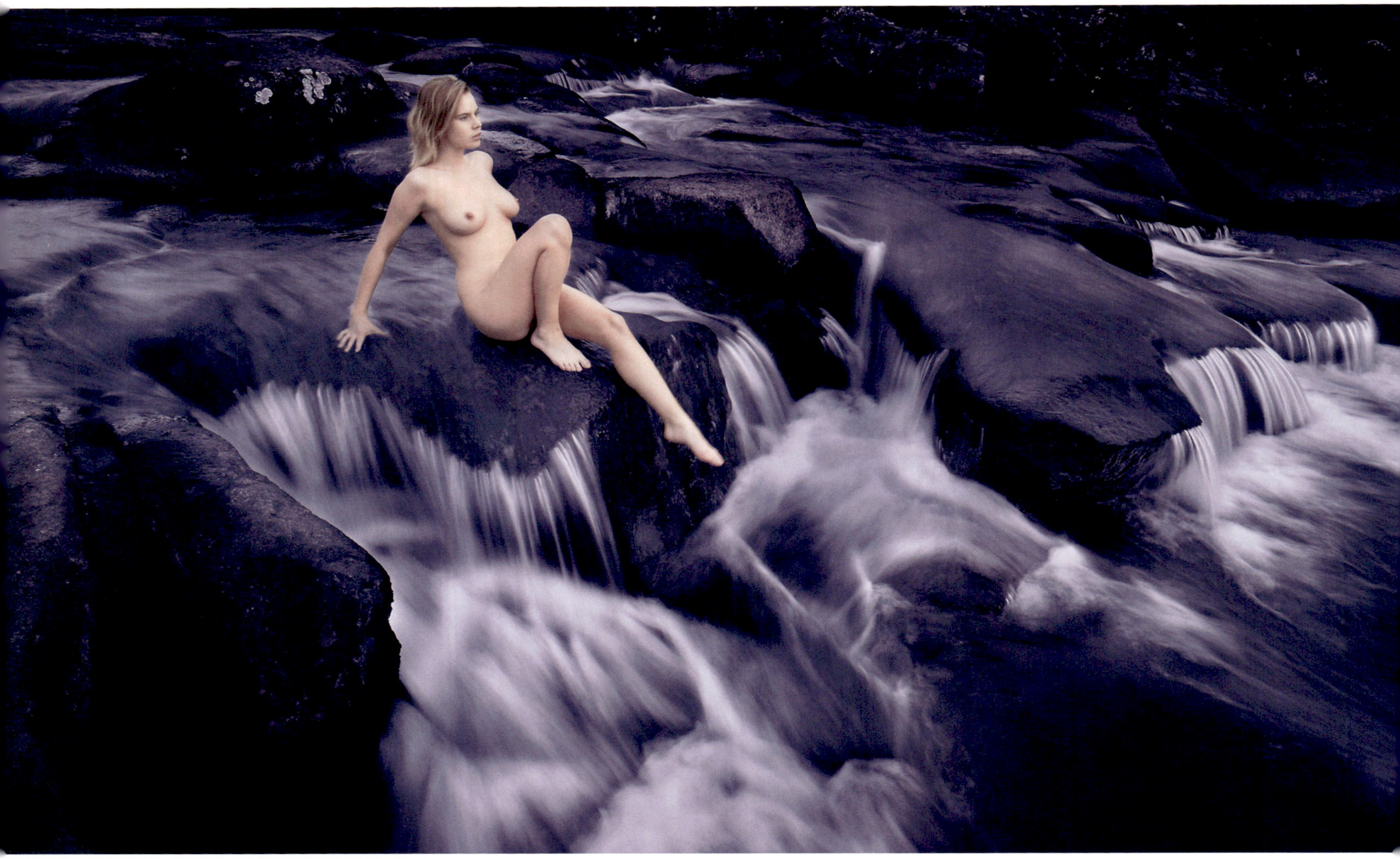

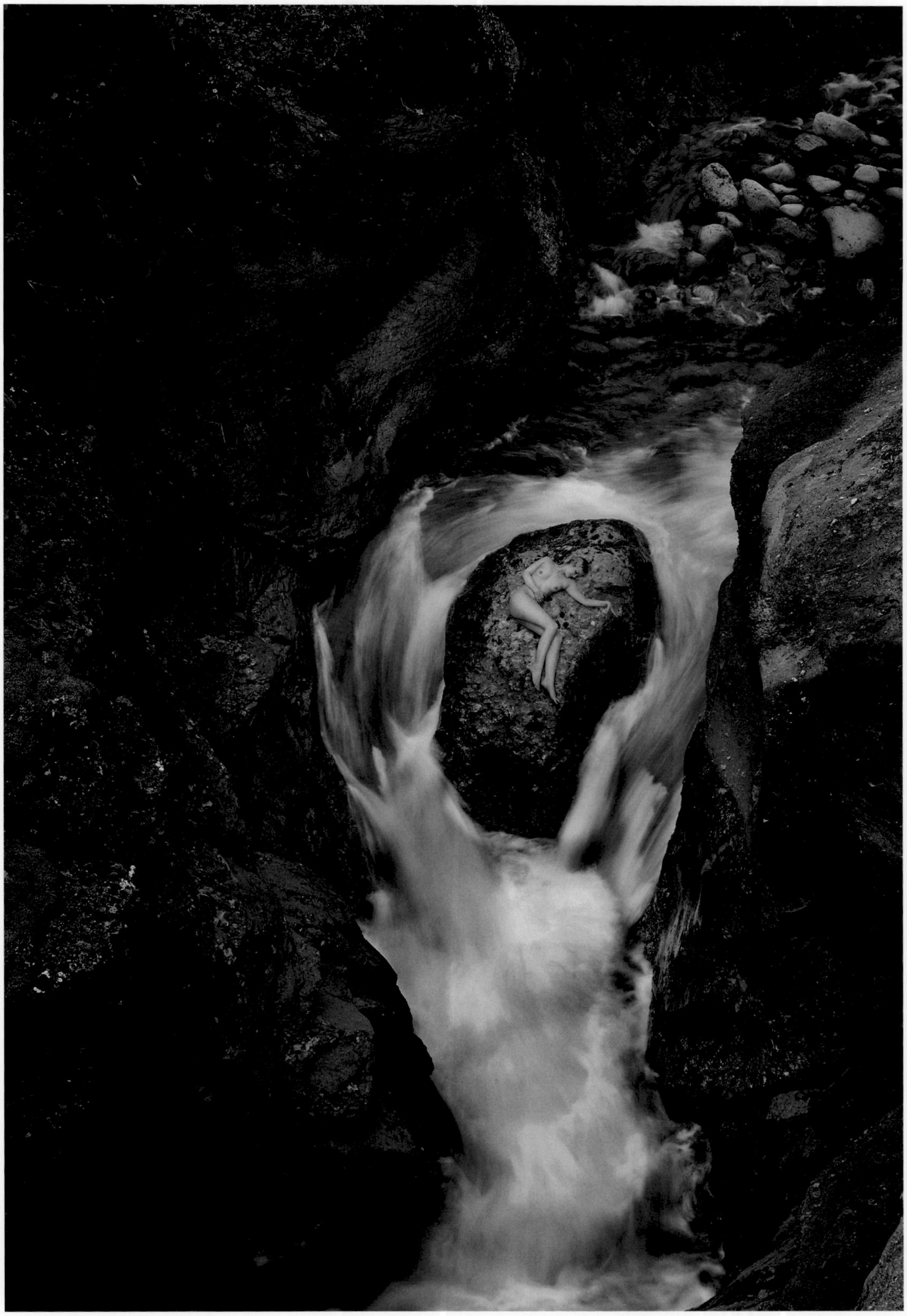

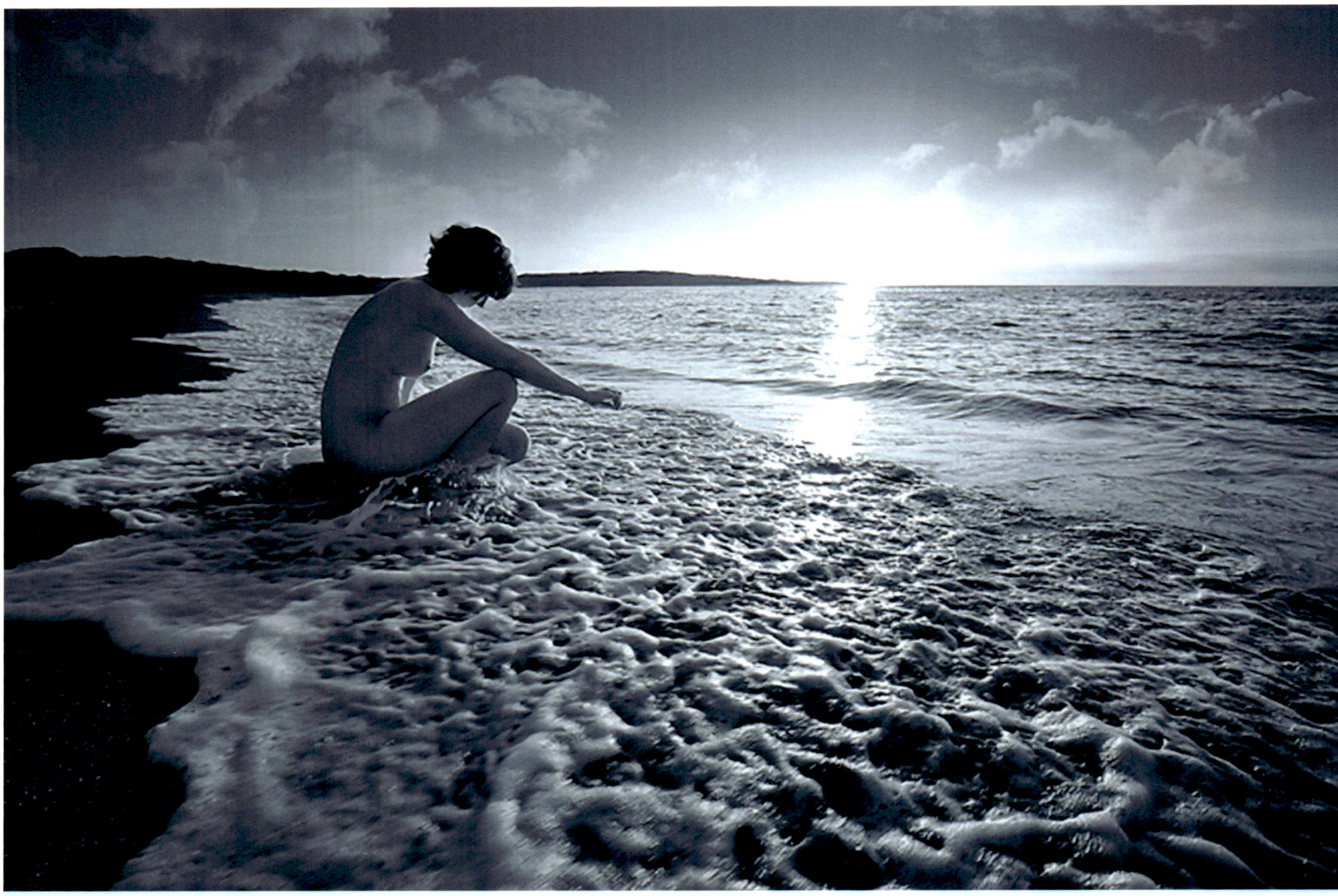

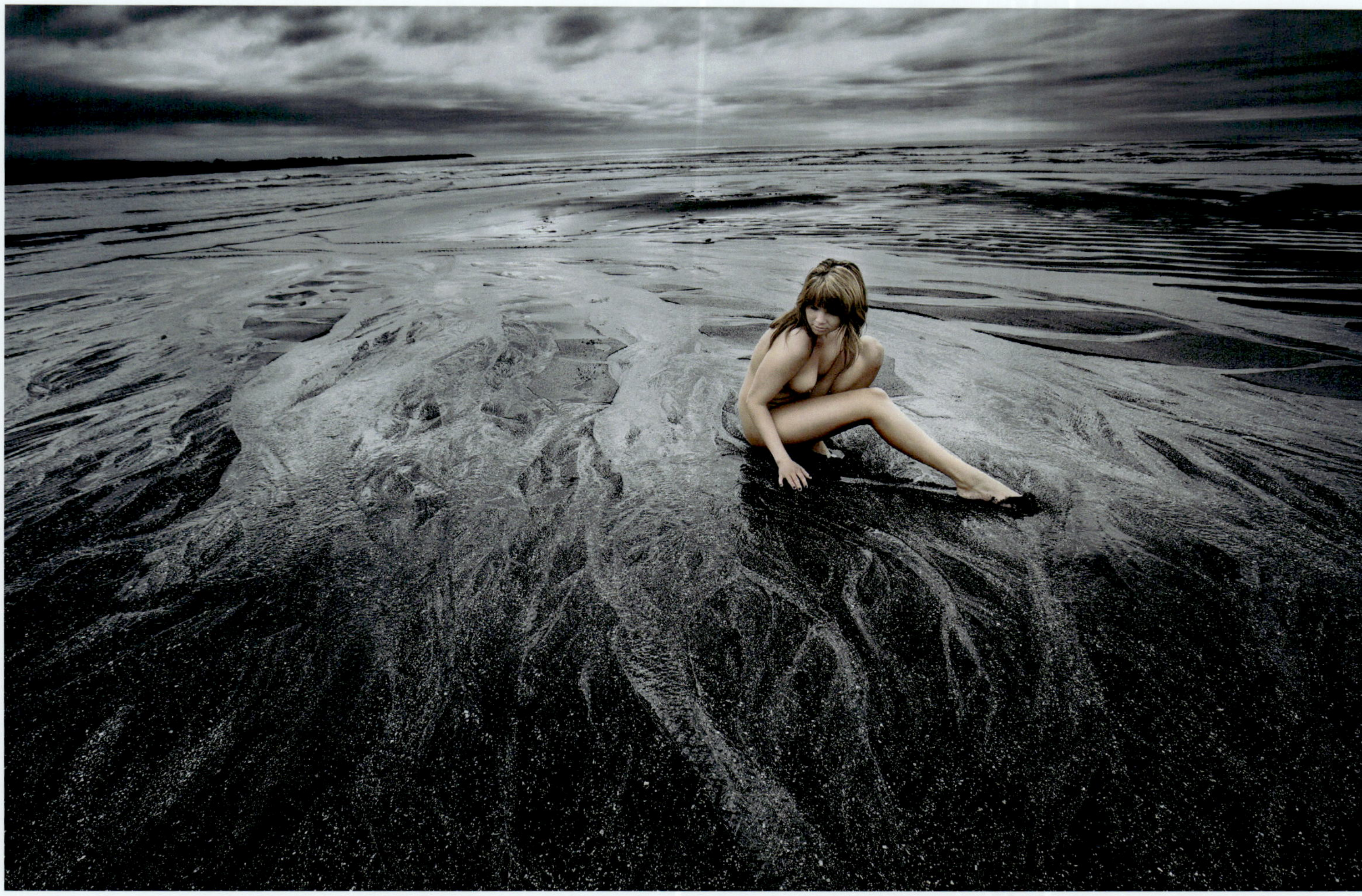

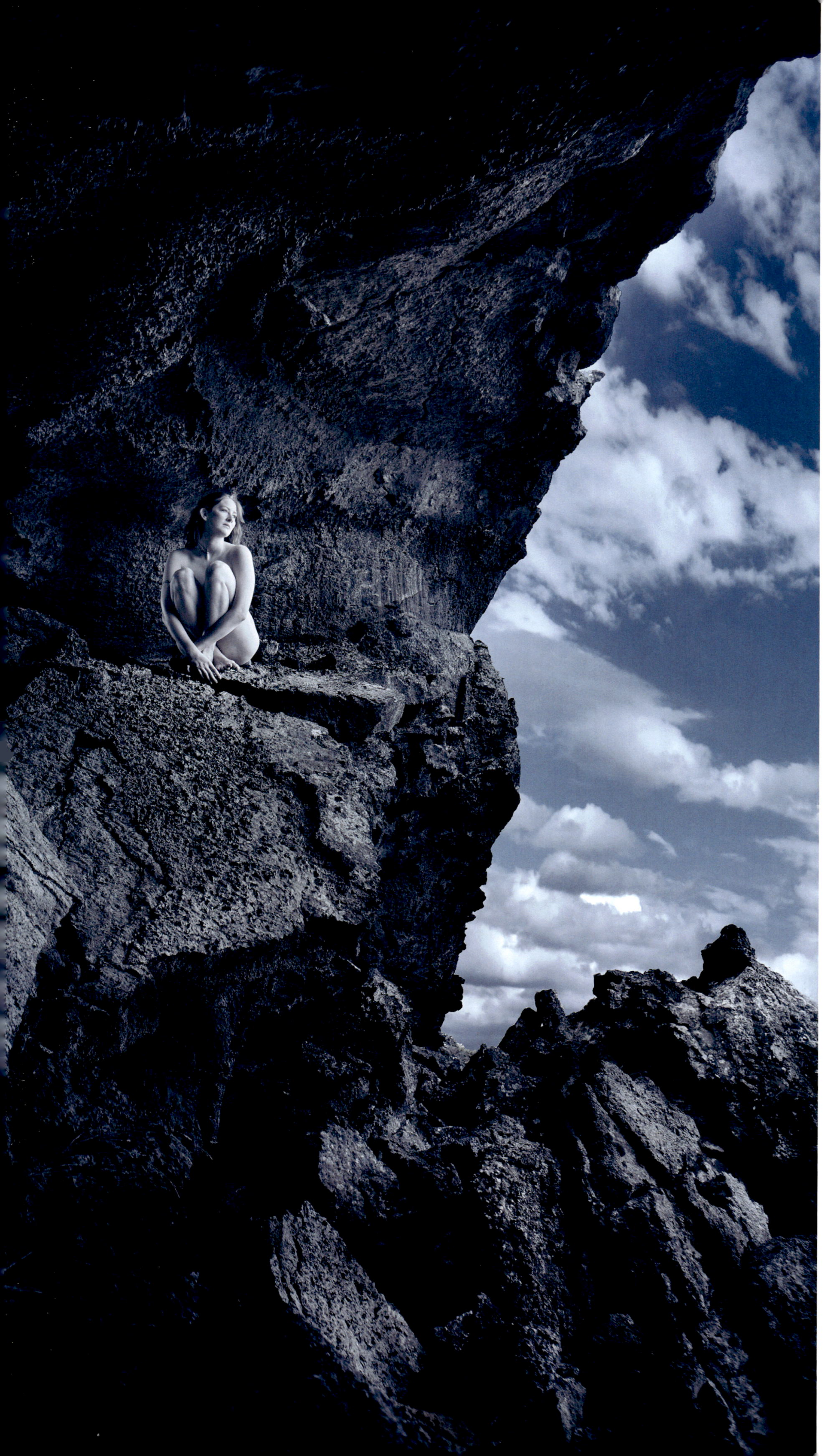

Bið

Meðan
ég bíð þín
ertu kær
eins og sumardagur

Þegar þú kemur
springa sóleyjar út
milli steinanna

Wait

While
I await you
you're as dear
as summer day

When you arrive
buttercups bloom
among the stones

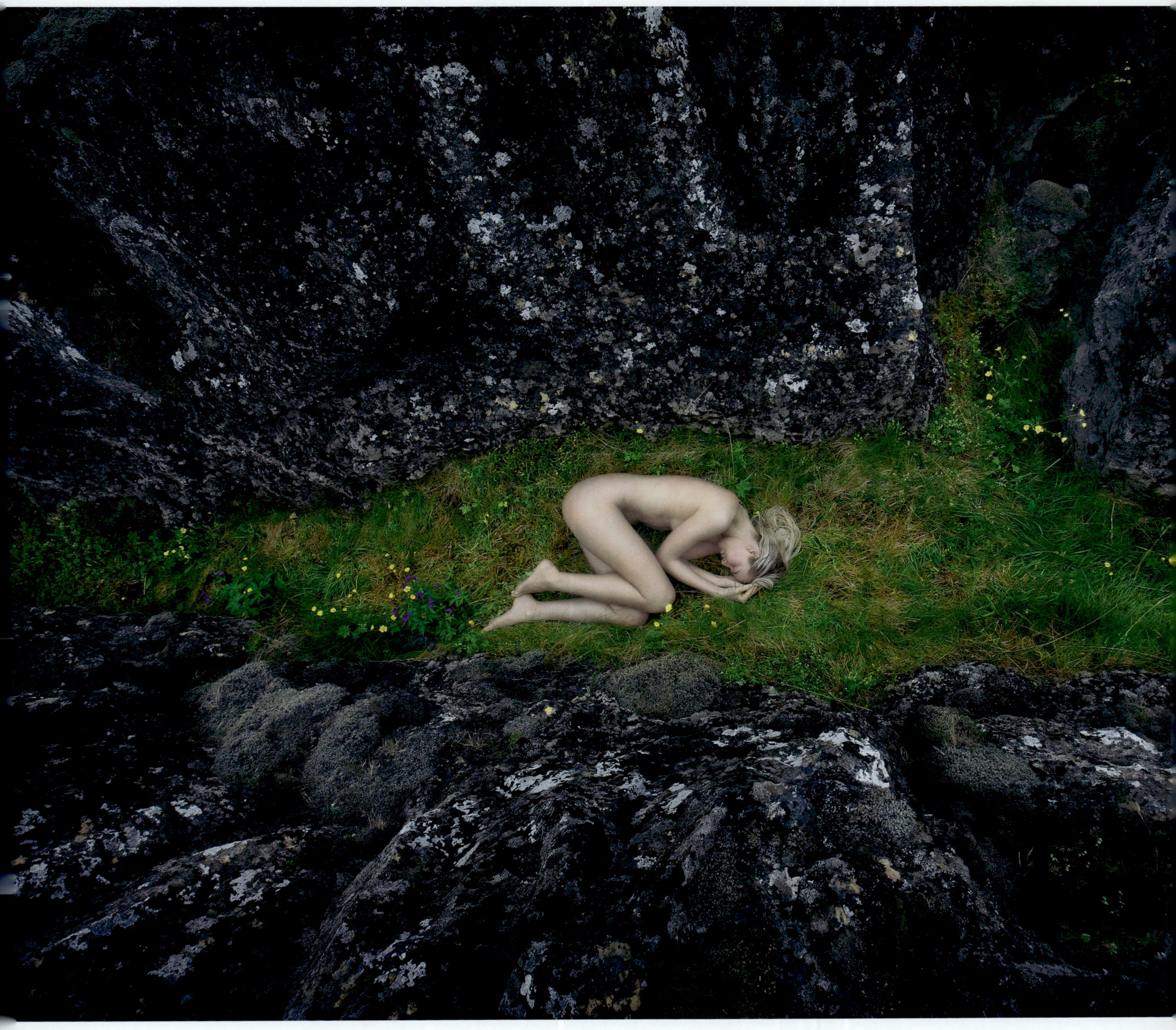

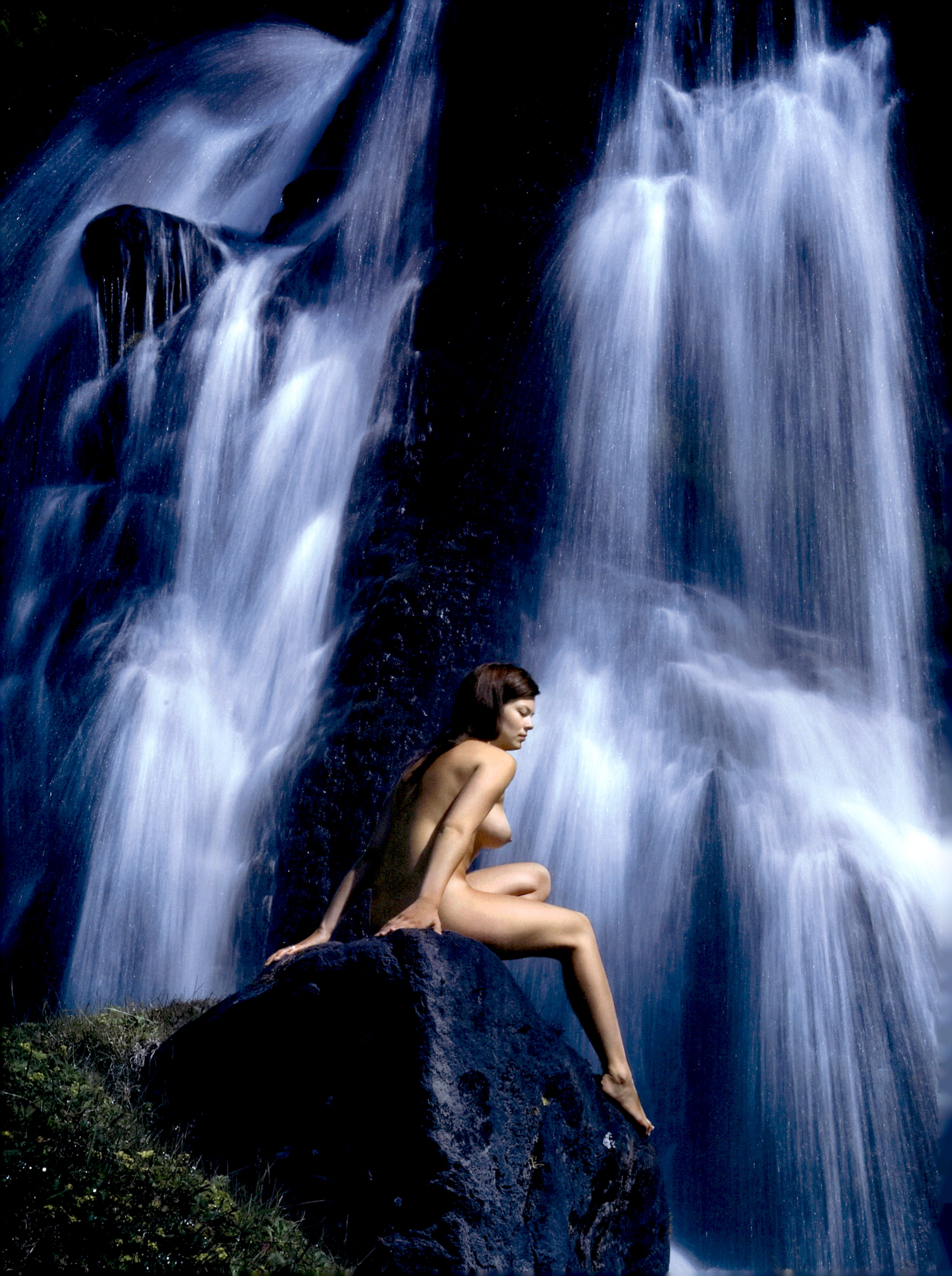

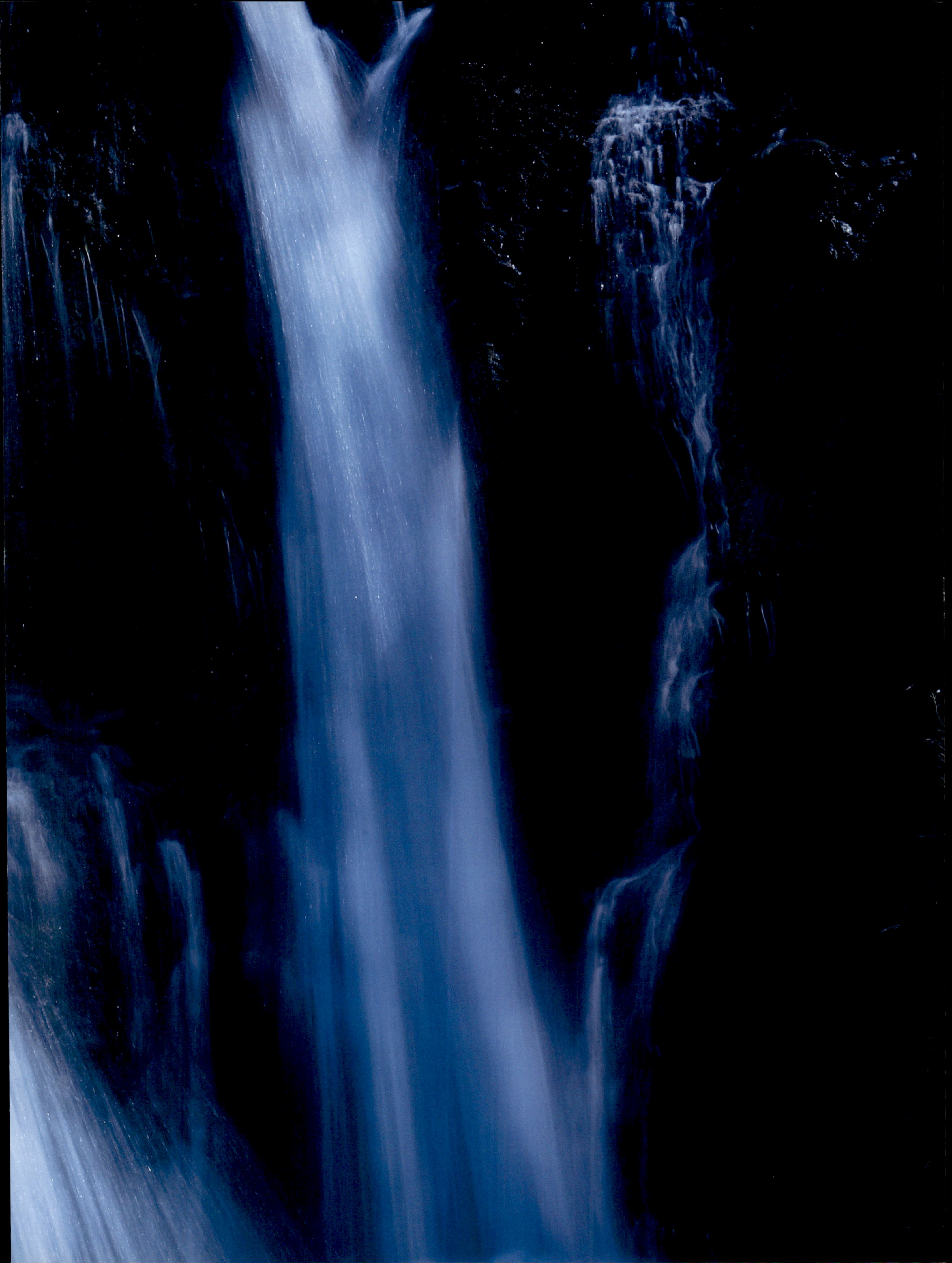

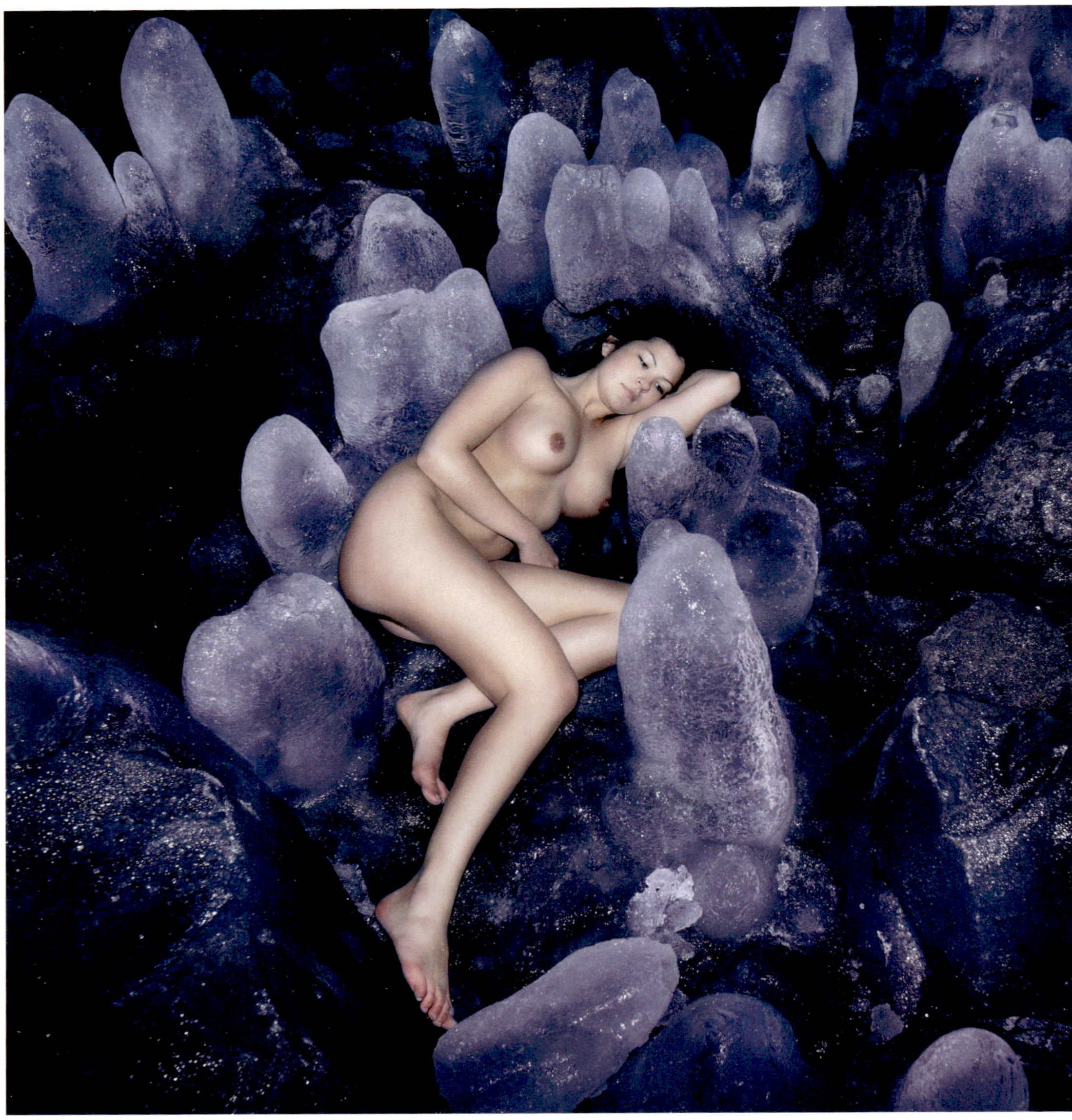

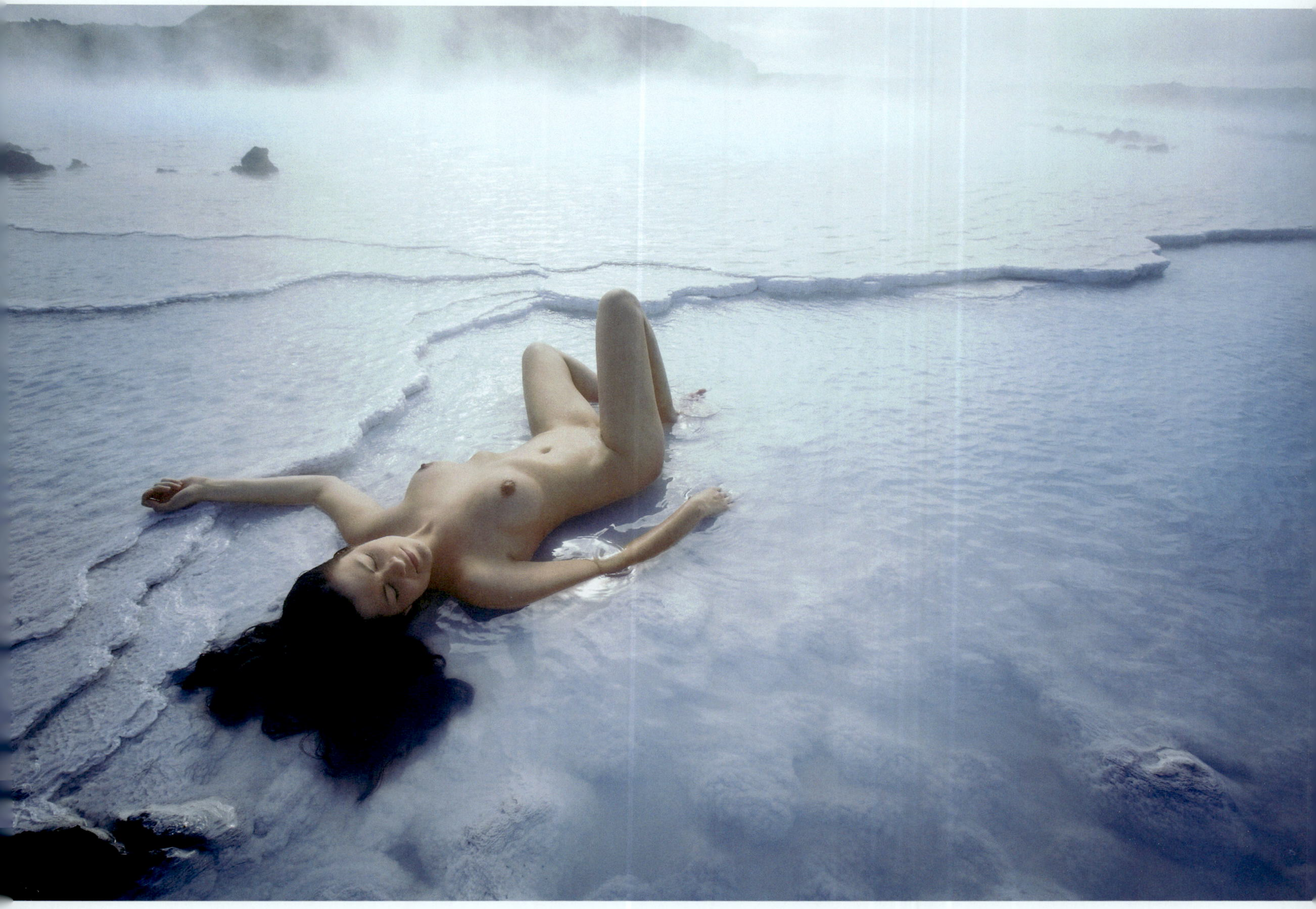

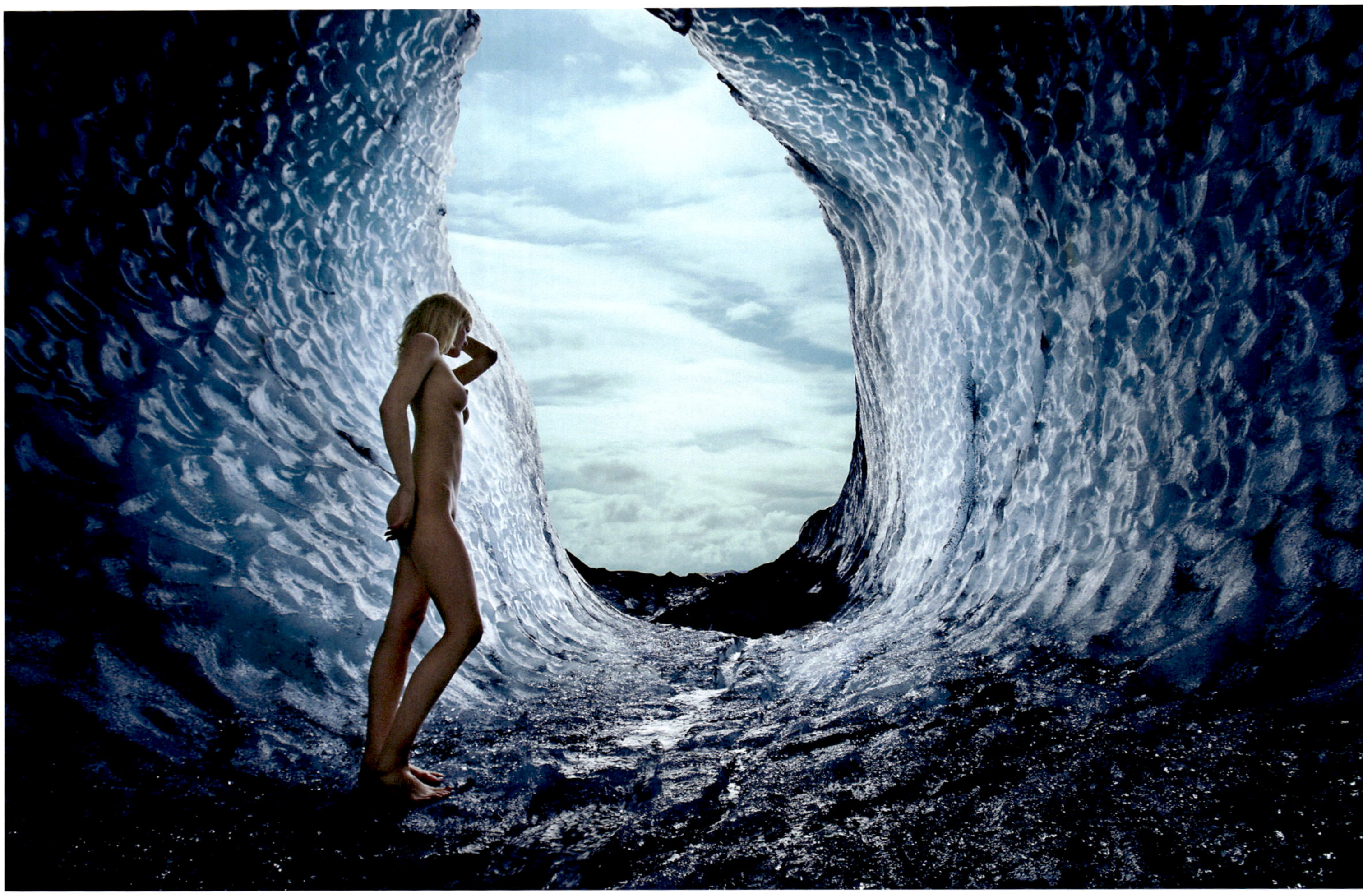

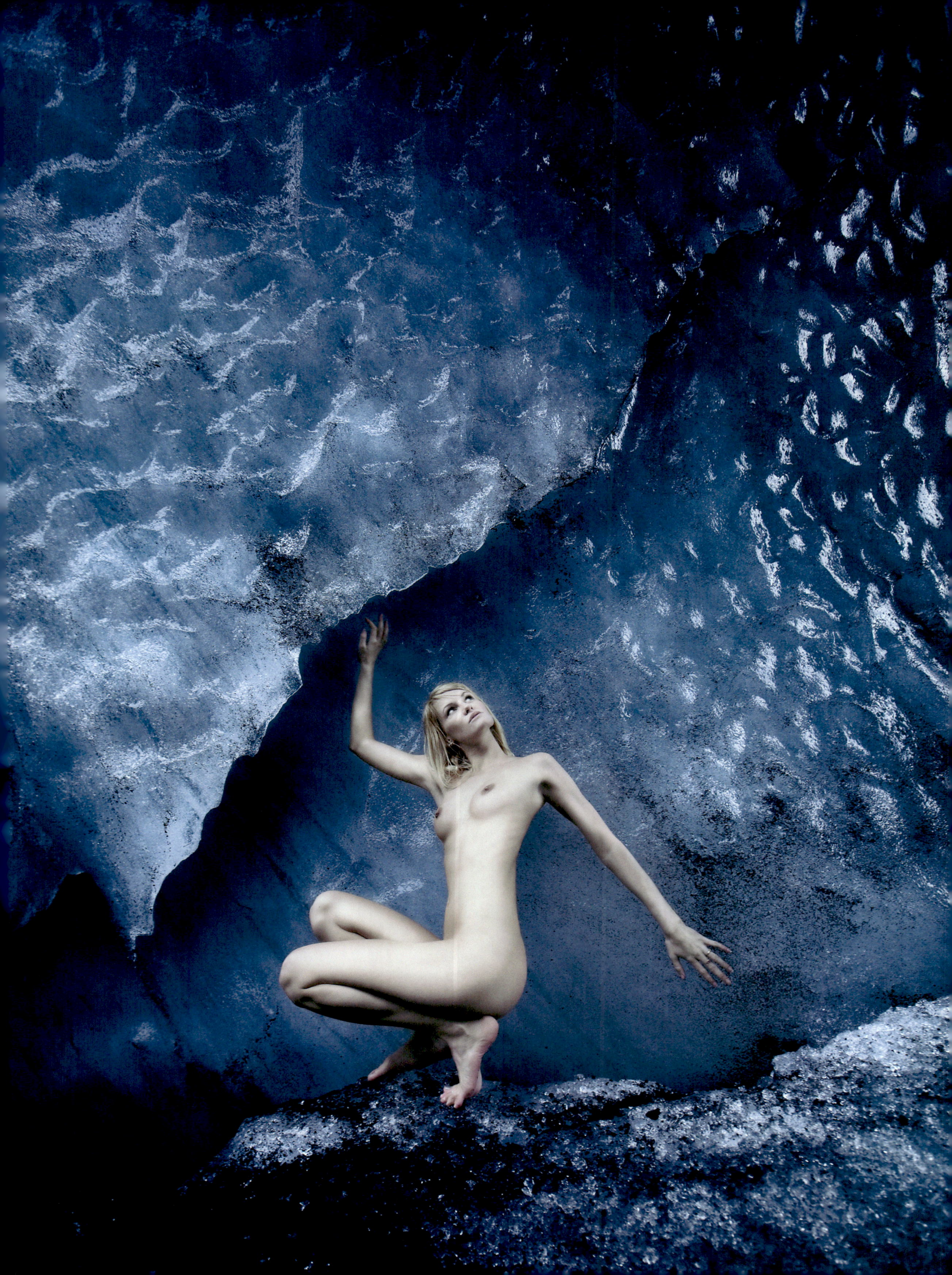

Mildi

Birtan þverr
seiðandi rökkrið
gerir alla fagra
jafnt steina og men

Gentleness

Light dwindles
the enchanting dusk
makes everything beautiful
stone as well as men

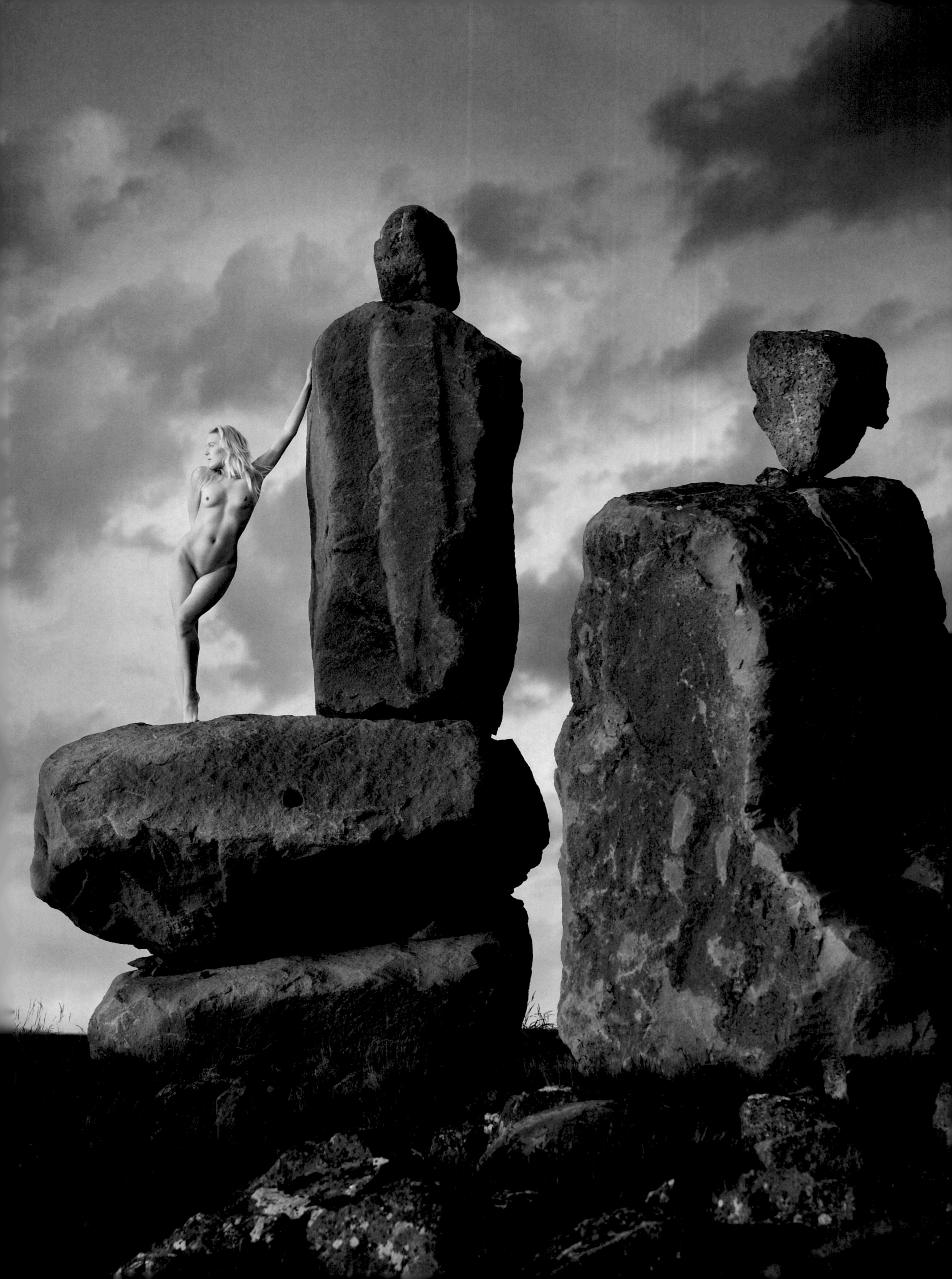

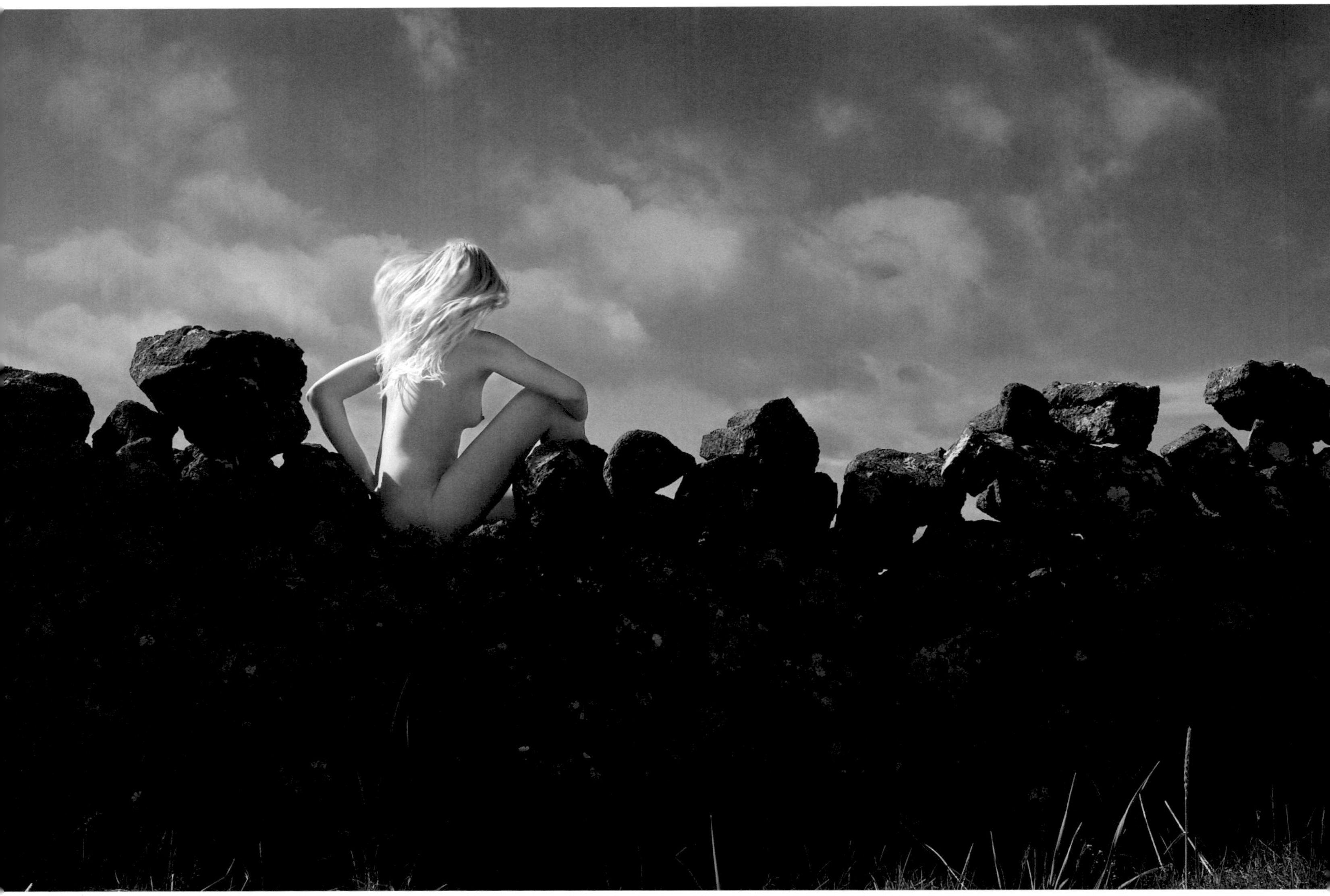

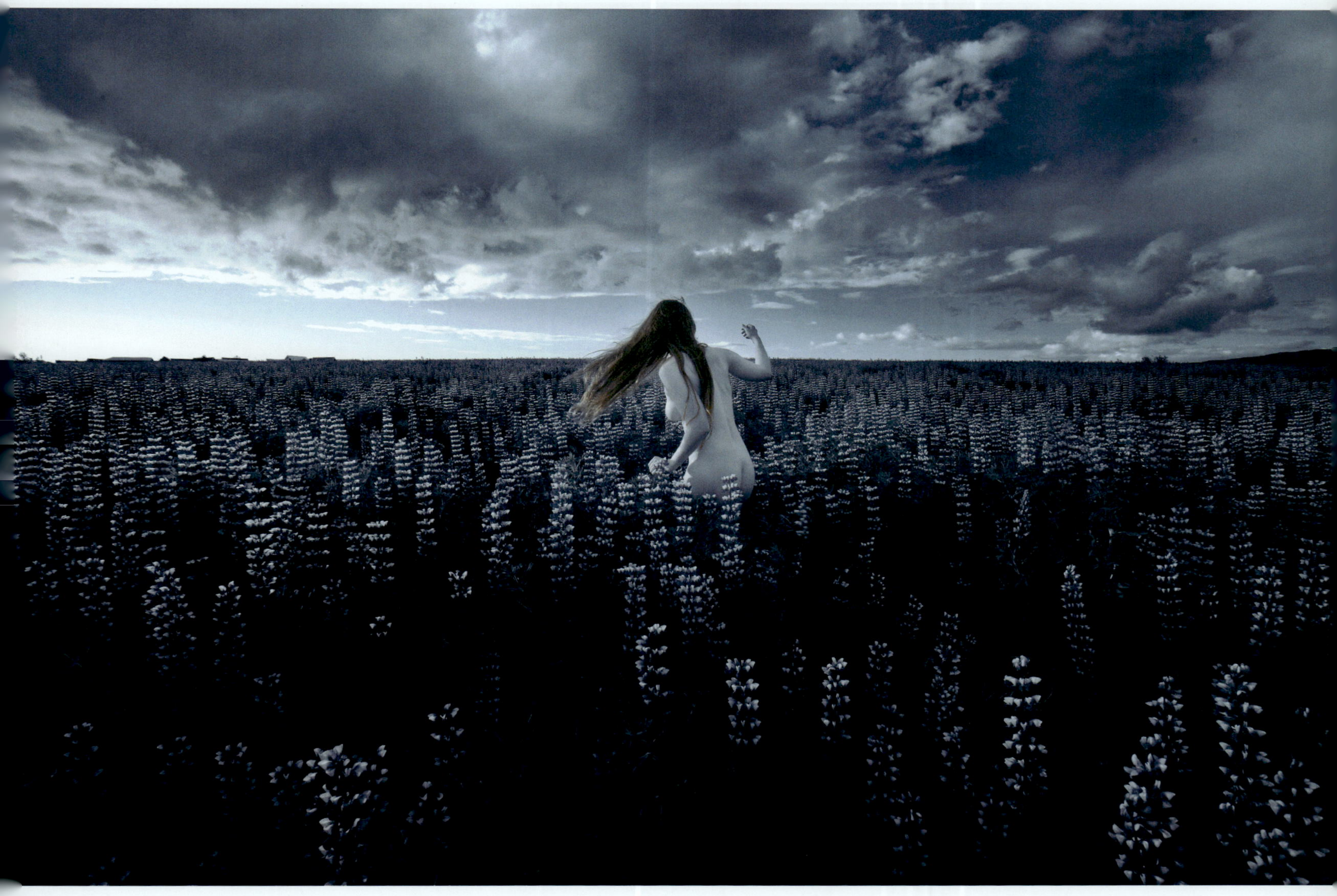

Blóm

Heiðarblóm
finnur skjól
hjá foldarsteini
festir rætur
hjúfrar sig að klettavegg

Vaxa blóm í grýttri urð
guðablóm fyrir augu mannanna

Flowers

The flower of the moor
finds itself a lee
by an earth-bound rock
takes root
huddles up a crag

Flowers grow in stony ground
God's own flowers for the eyes of humans

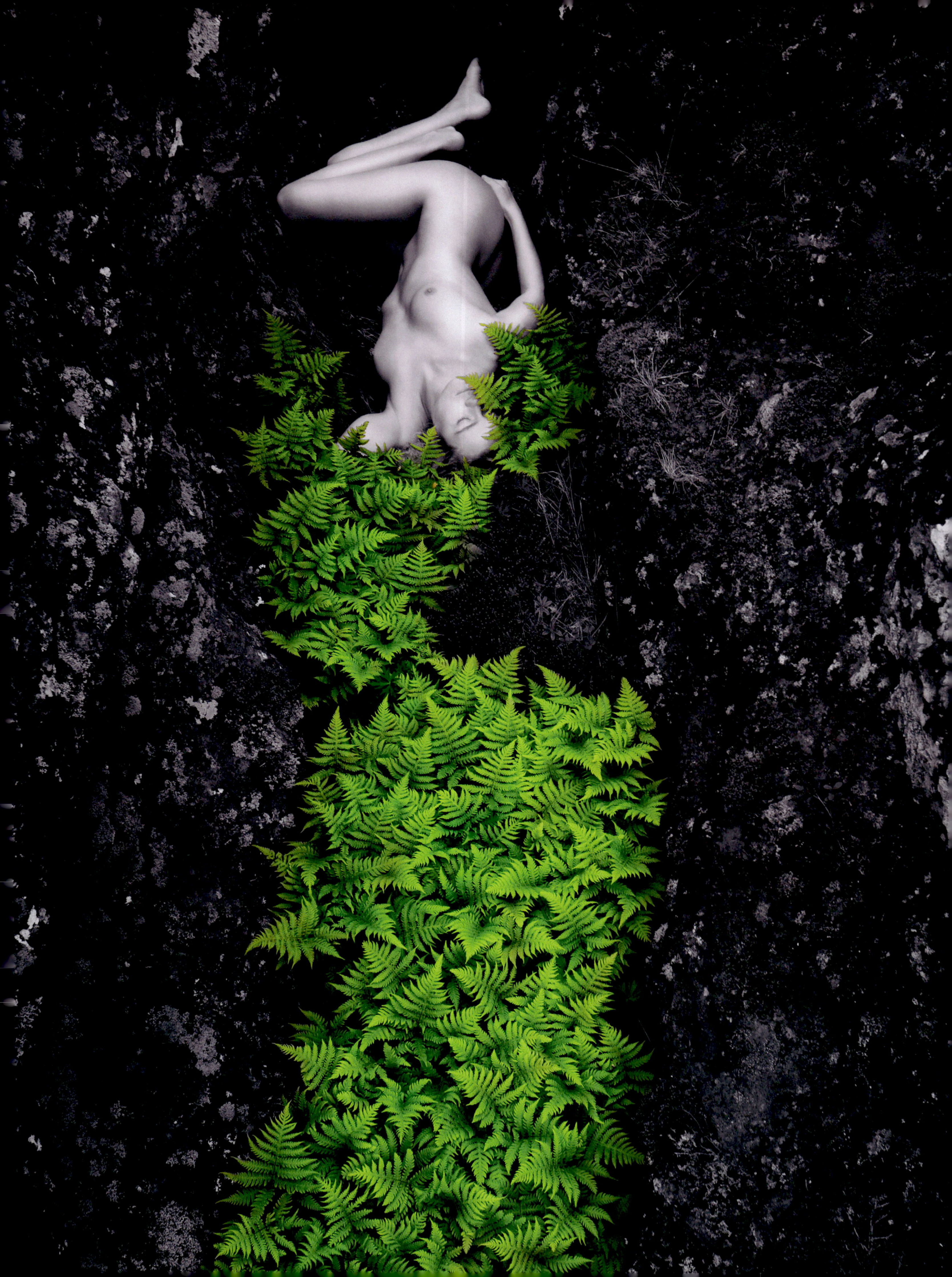

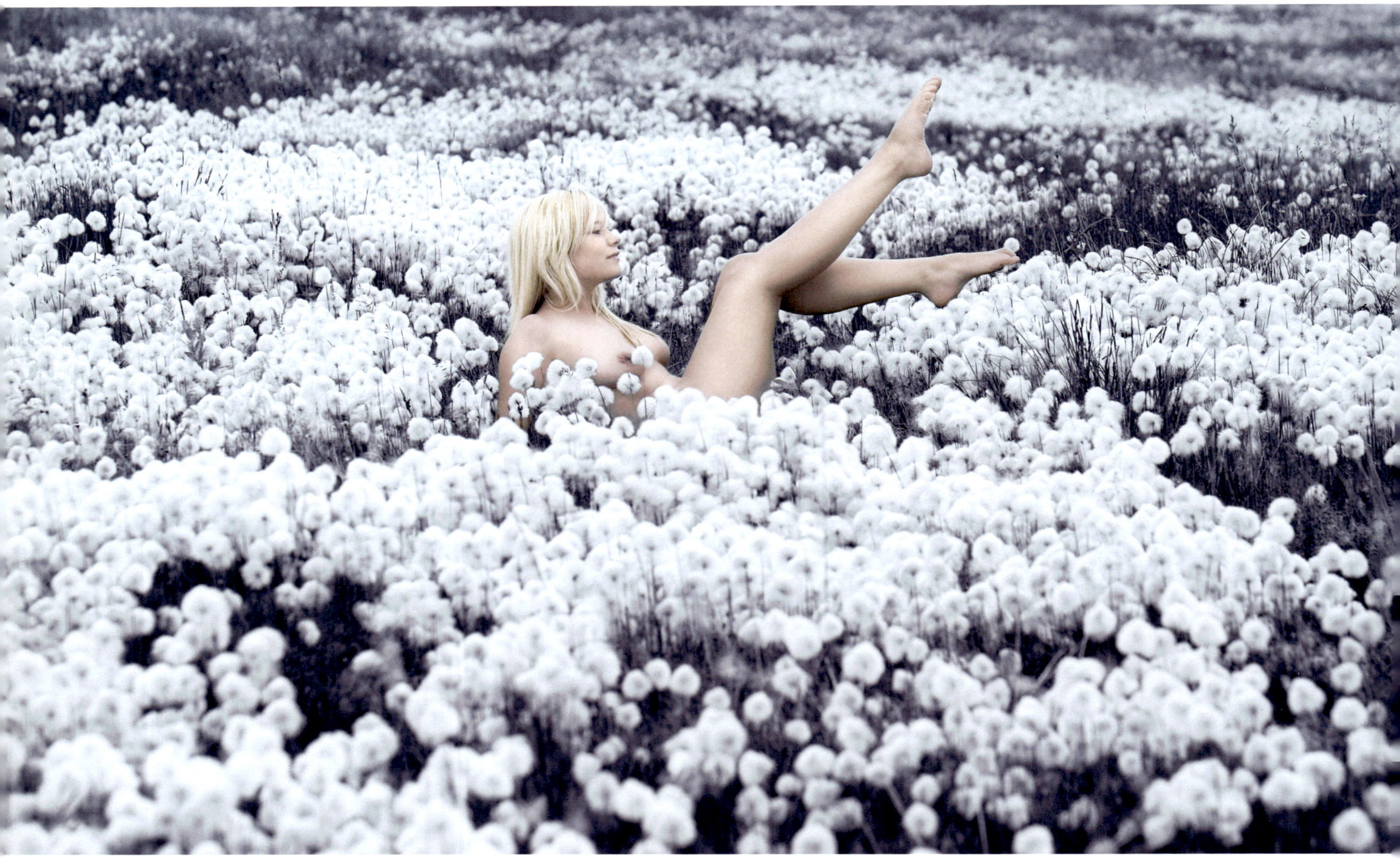

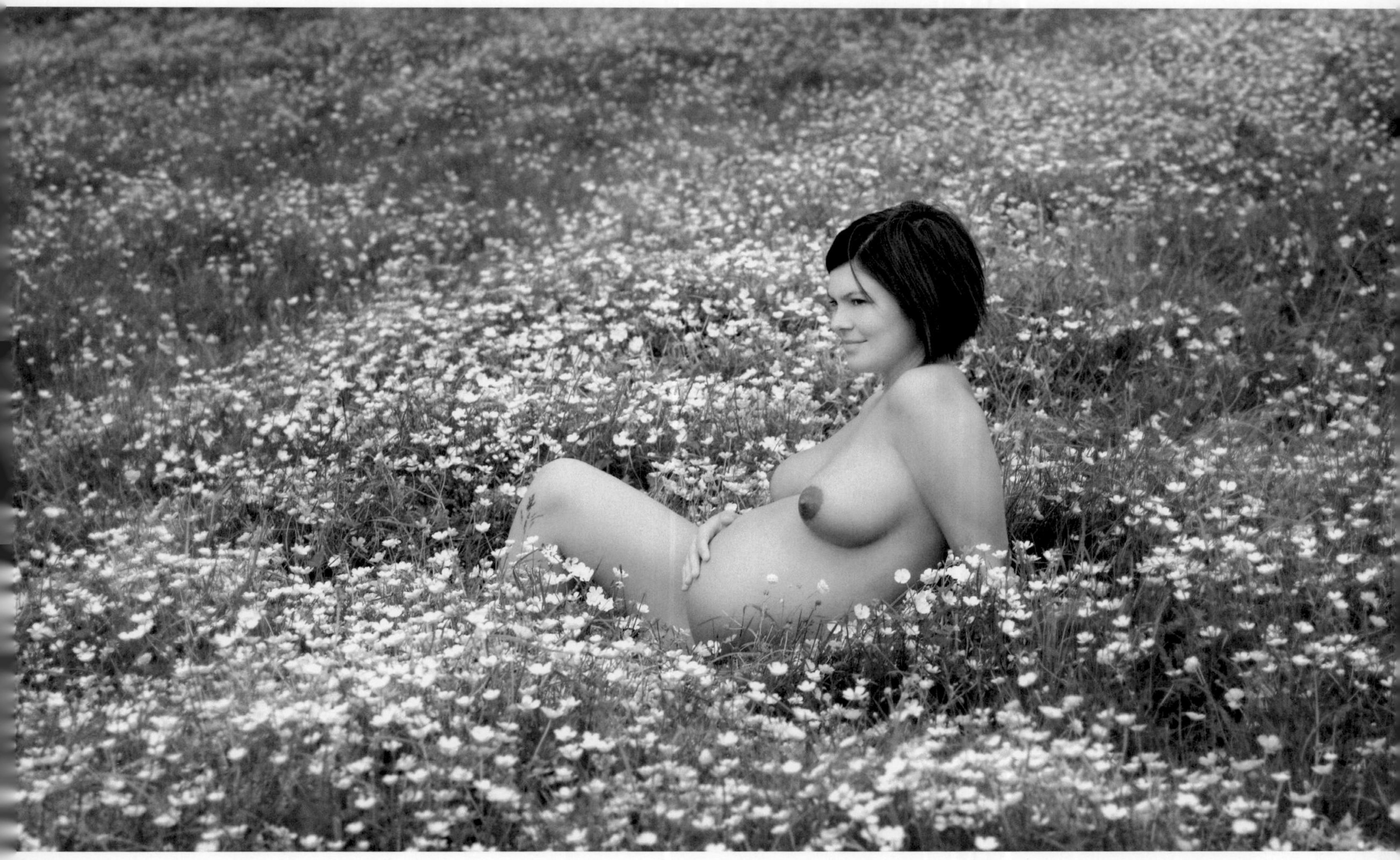

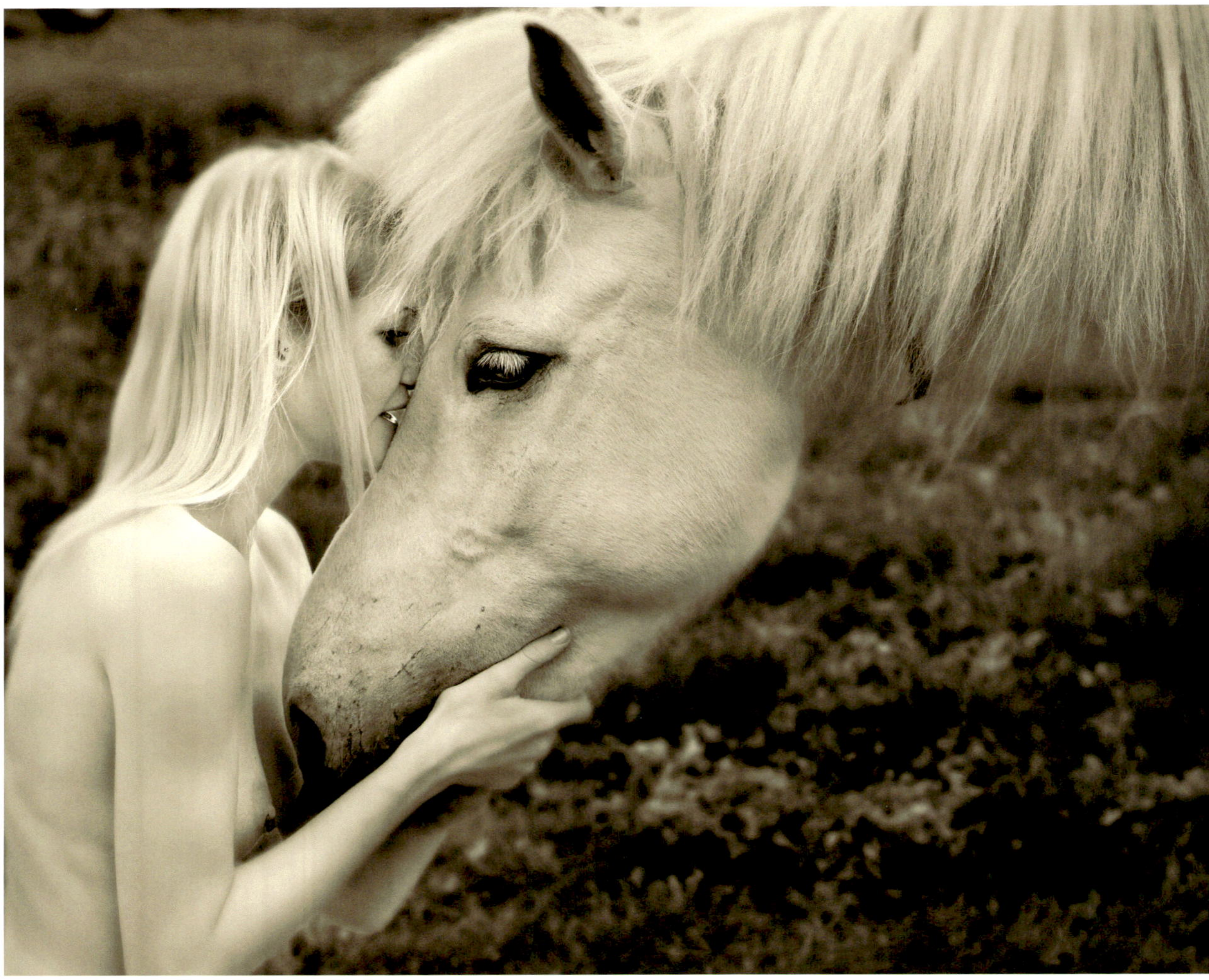

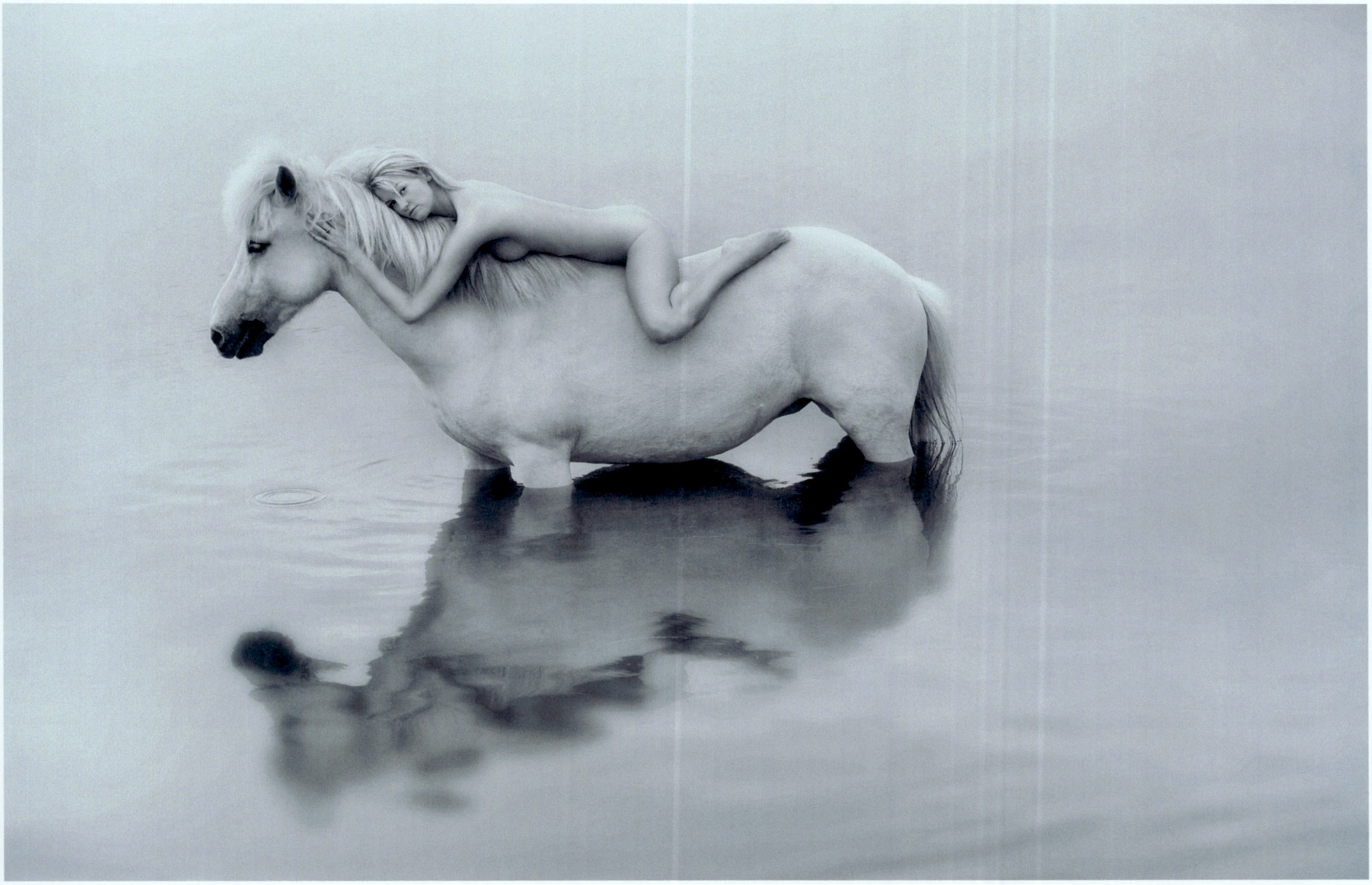

Af moldu	**From Dust**
Nú hvílir hún	Now she rests
í garðinum	in the garden
hvílir hún	rests
í vindinum	in the wind
með sumarblóm	with summer flowers
og heiðarkvist	and a twig of heather
á brjóstinu	on her chest

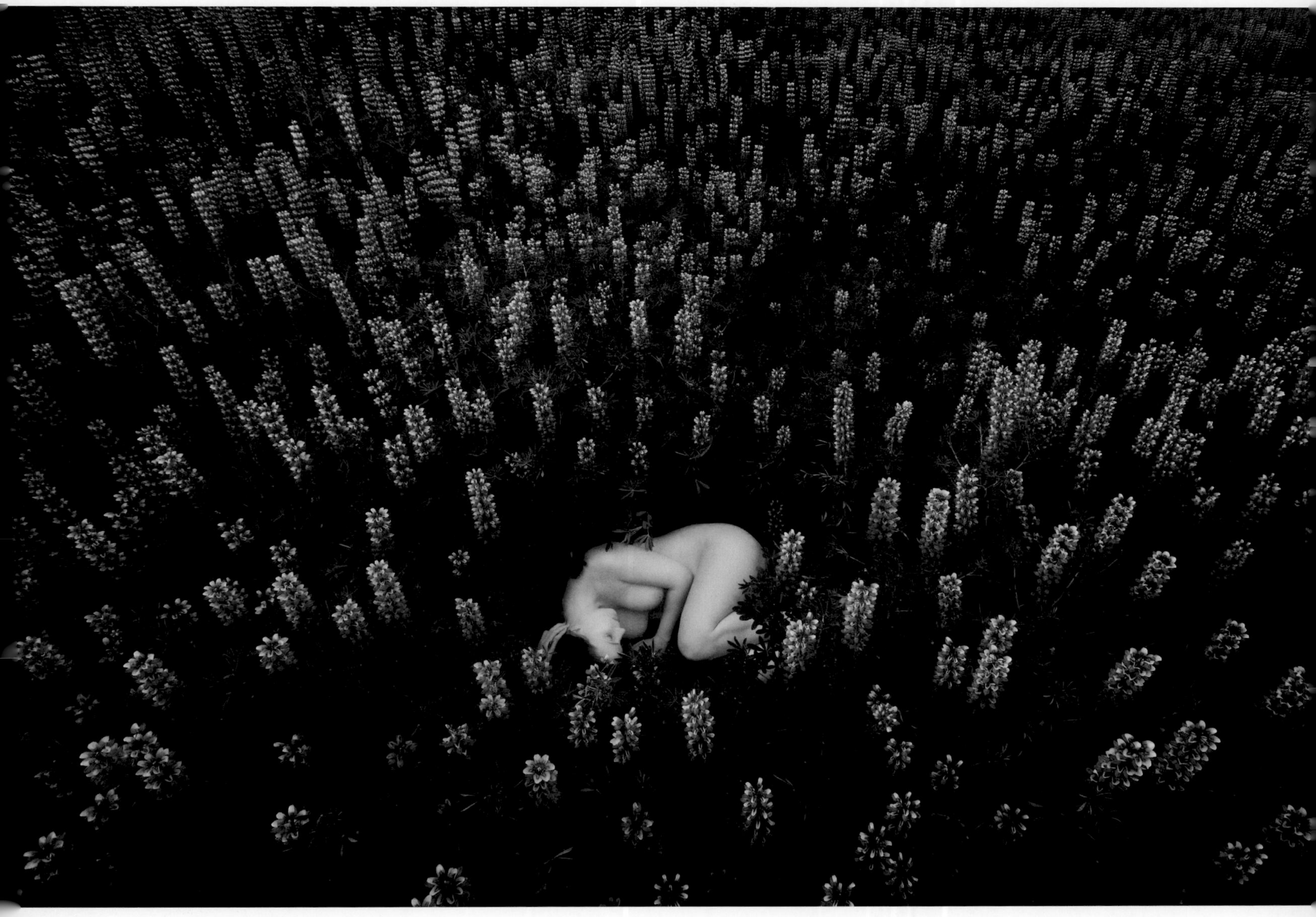

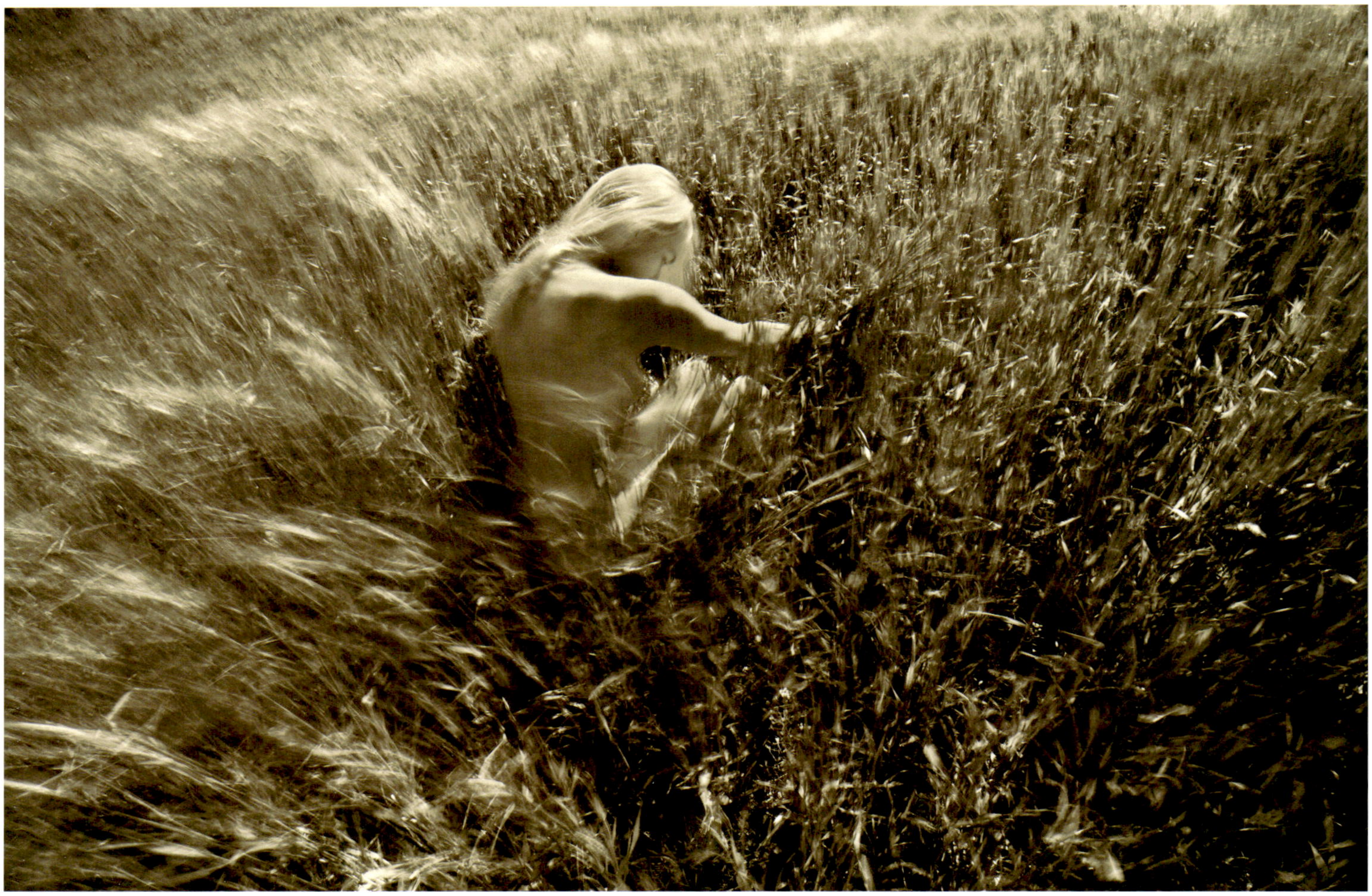

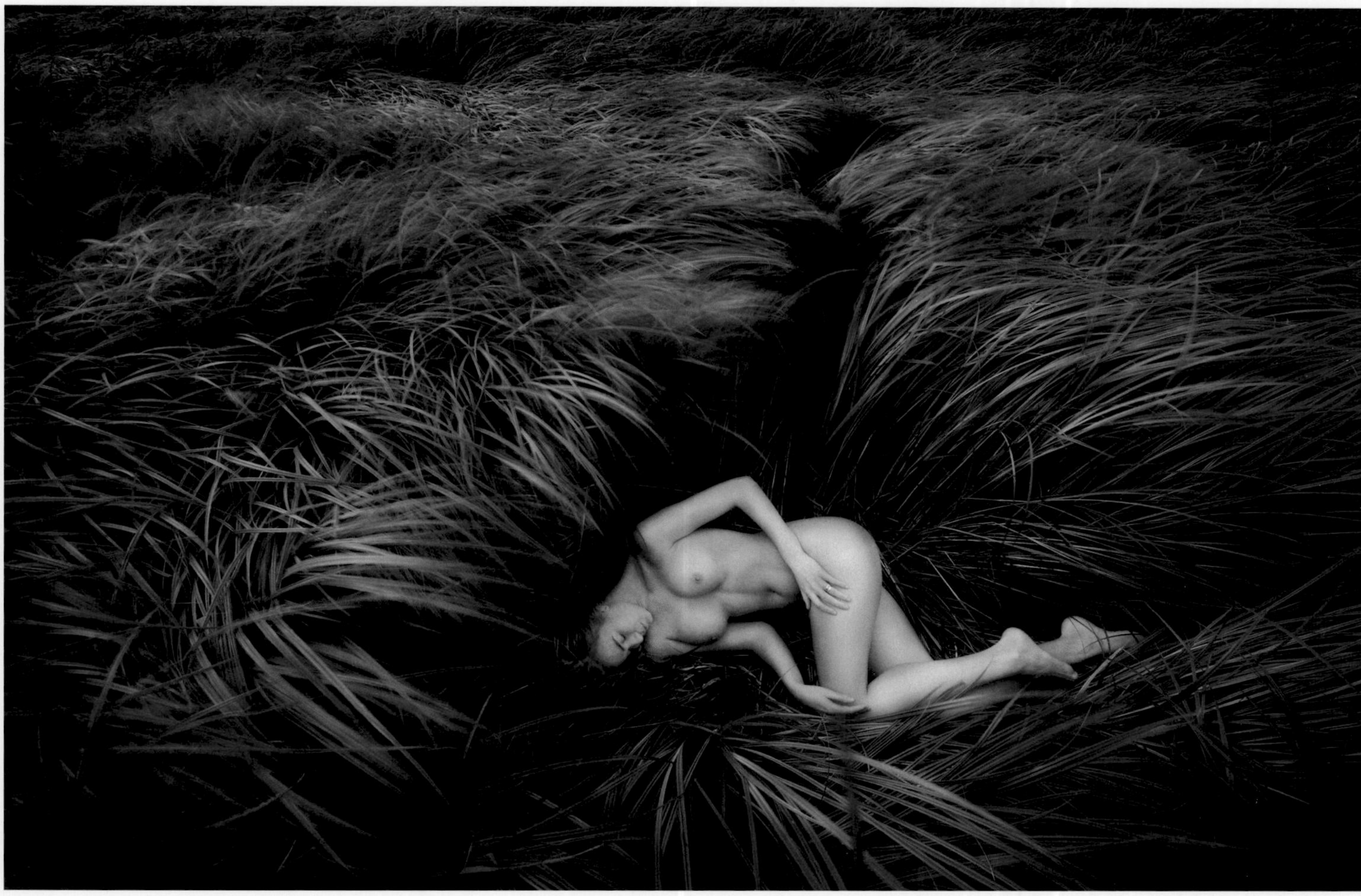

Nótt

Við
í þessari nótt
týnd
í þessum heimi
Finnumst aldrei framar
fyrsta sinni

Night

We
in this night
lost
in this world
Never again find each other
for the first time

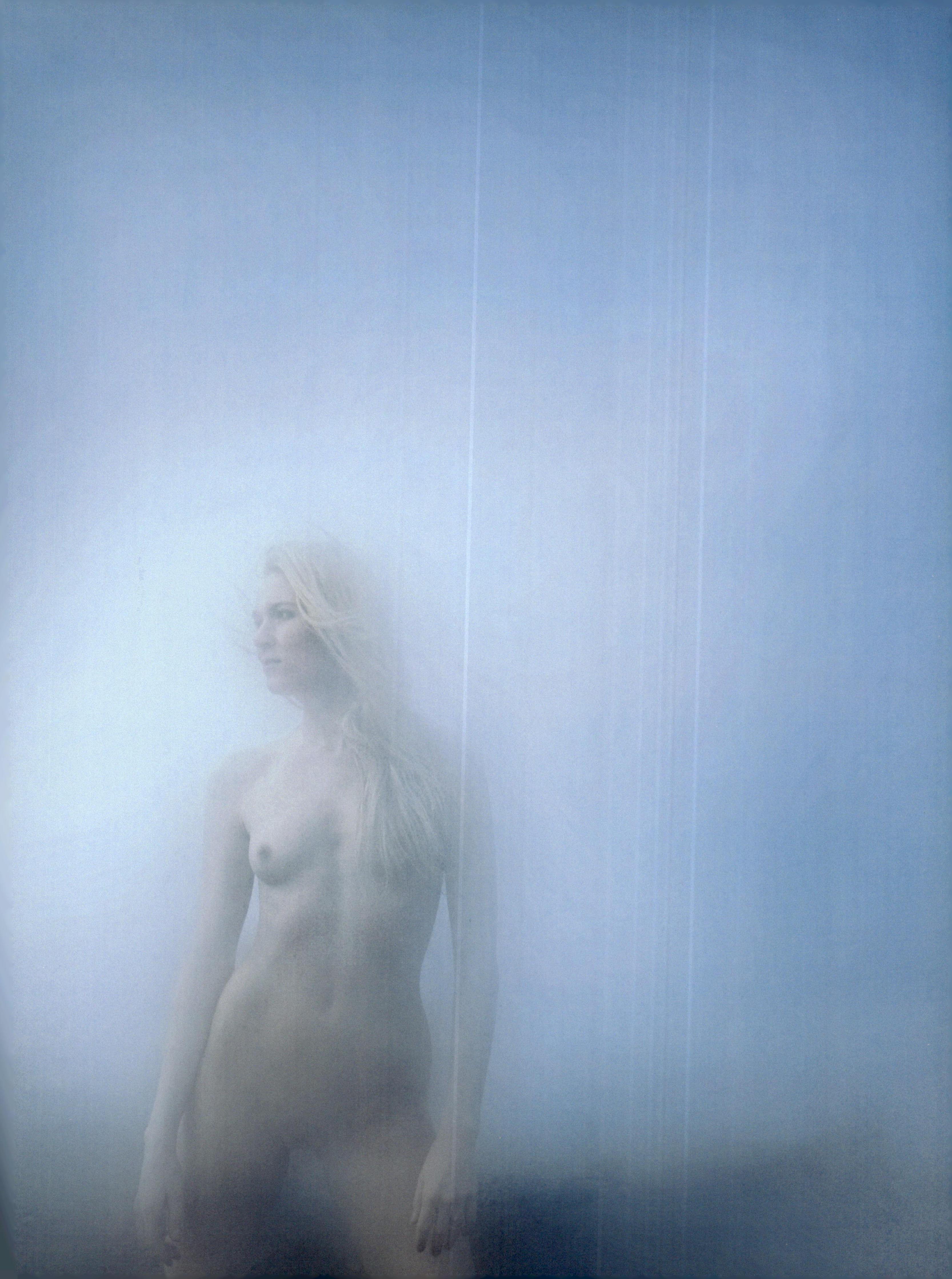

Beyond Bare Landscapes

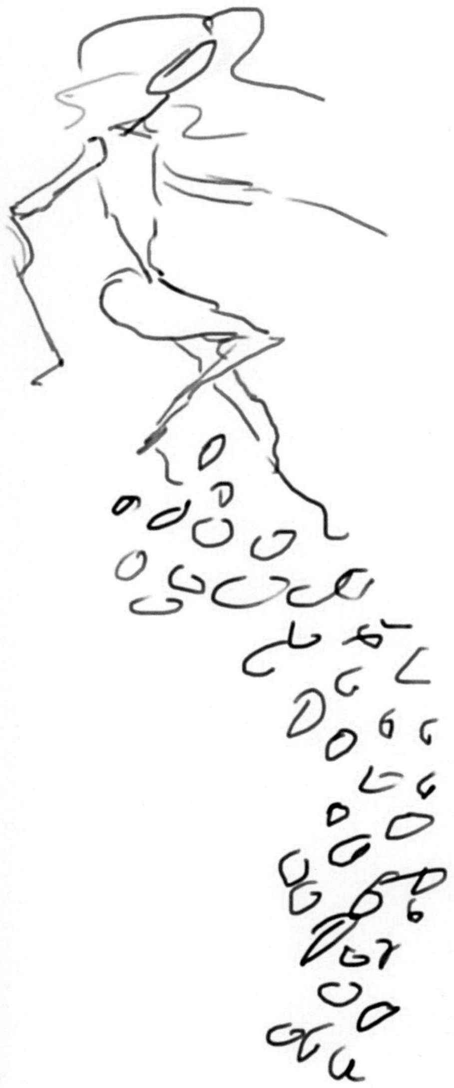

The genesis of Bare Landscapes came to me while I was re-working some old images that I had shot on film. One photo in particular stood out from the others. It was a picture of a nude woman that I had taken some years before in Iceland. In the photo the model is posed in a quarry of dark rock. I had always loved that shot because of the simplicity of the elements and the contrasts they presented. That photo ignited my first thoughts about the possibility of creating a book with nudes set against natural landscapes. The more I thought about the photo, the more I realized Iceland was the perfect place to capture those images. For one, I knew the land well; I had grown up there and I was aware of how special the terrain was. It had a very unique topography with uncommon textures and a light that I hadn't seen anywhere else. In addition, most of the nature there was untouched and that seemed a good ingredient to partner up with the natural beauty of the Icelandic women. The potential of putting them together intrigued me artistically.

From that single shot I started to develop the project. From the beginning, I wanted the book to be a visual experience and I envisioned the images accompanied by poems. Like all artistic seeds, my thoughts for the book started to blossom. I began to make a list of locations and how the models would be posed in them. At the same time it was important that the nudes be organic to the landscape, compliment it, but also be as natural as the flowers and fauna that grew from the earth. I wanted to see Iceland with new eyes and to translate that freshness into my photos.

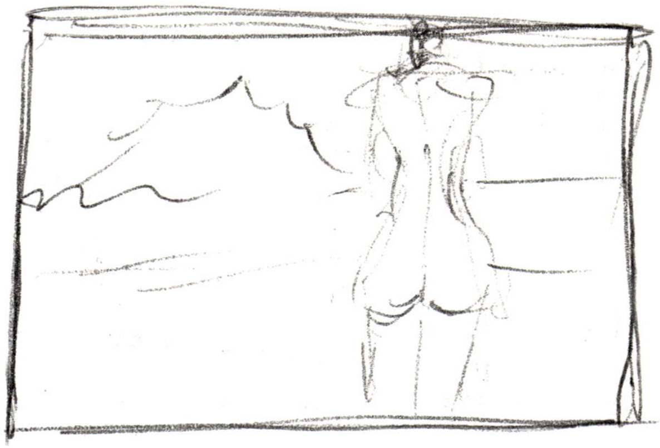

When I think about creating an image, I often sketch it out beforehand. For me, it is a form of brainstorming, a way of playing with shapes and forms. Because I live in Los Angeles, I had to sketch from memory. I would imagine different poses for the models that would work with particular elements in each environment: water, ice, sand, and rock.

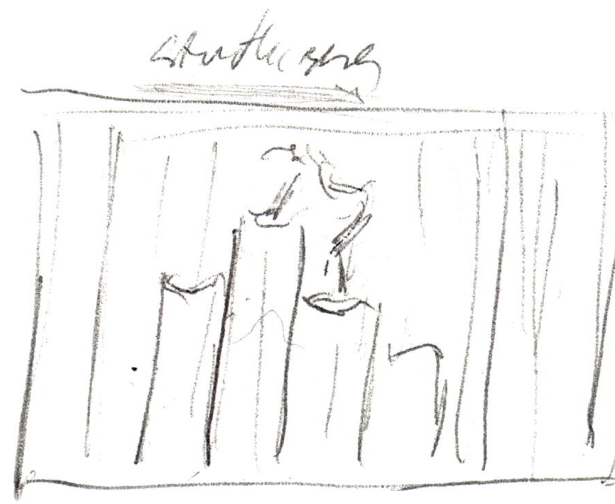

Some sketches matched a particular location, because I'd already been there. In these cases it was relatively easy to previsualize the image. Other times I would have to find new places that fit my ideas.

Iceland was formed by volcanic eruptions and shaped by the elements over time; both these factors have left many interesting and individual land formations. My idea was to get a little closer to the earth rather than just photograph the scenery. I wanted to see and feel the essence of the landscape and contrast it with the female form in a way that felt both primal and organic. Particularly, I wanted to show the harmony of nature integrated with the figure of a nude by juxtaposing both in the play of texture and form with light and shadow.

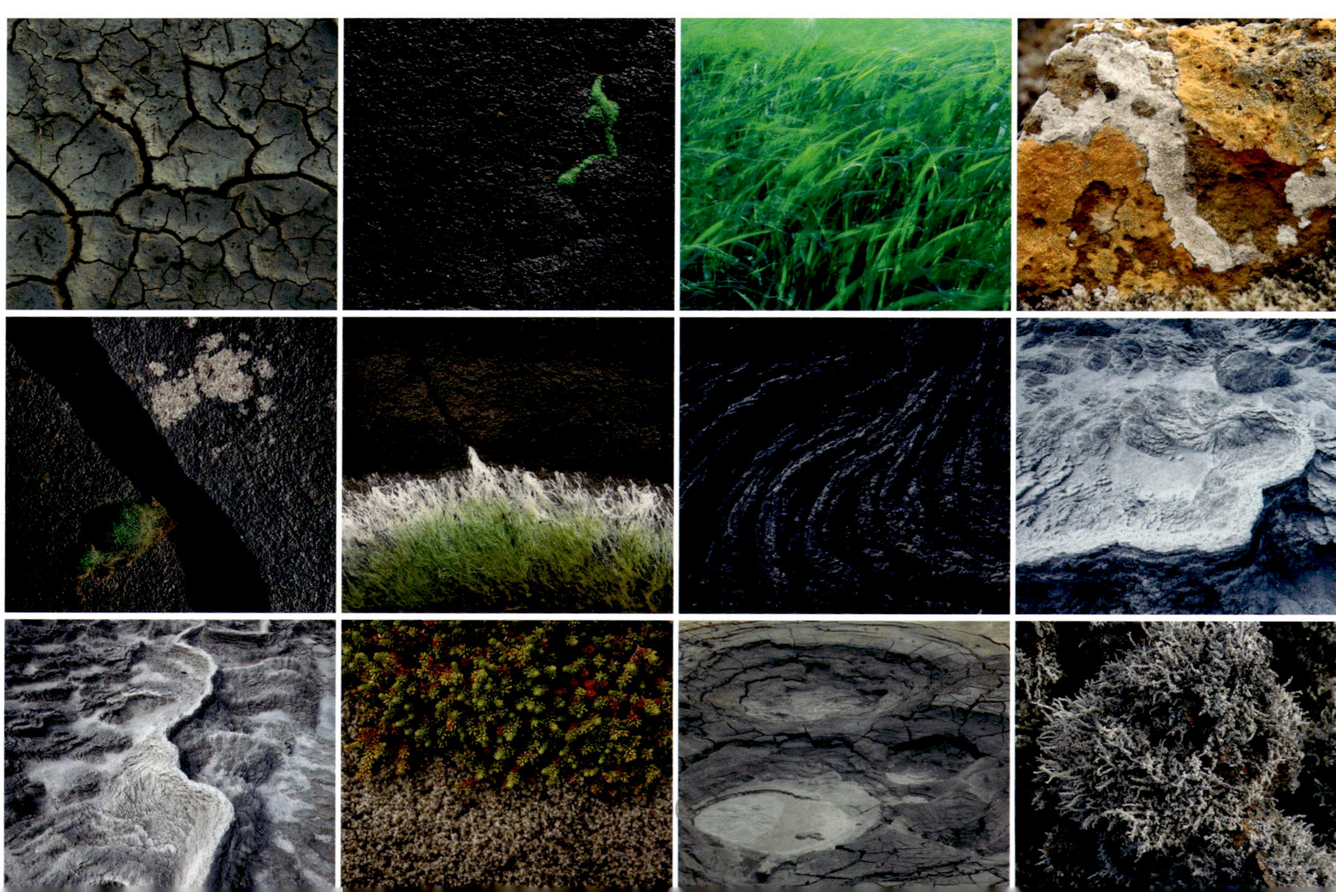

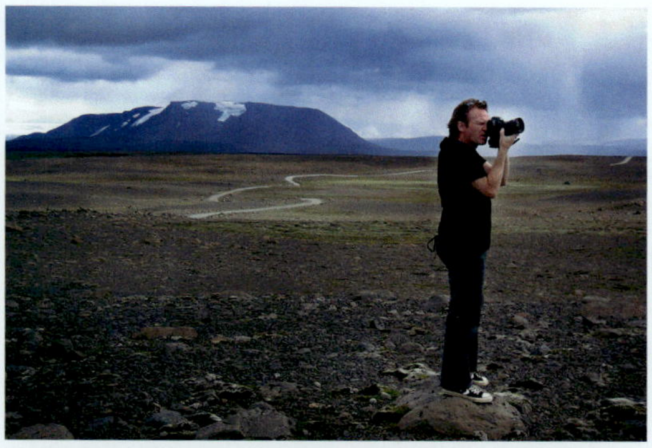

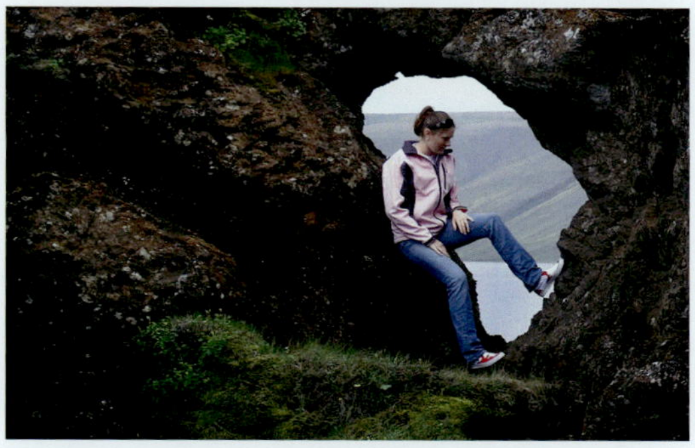

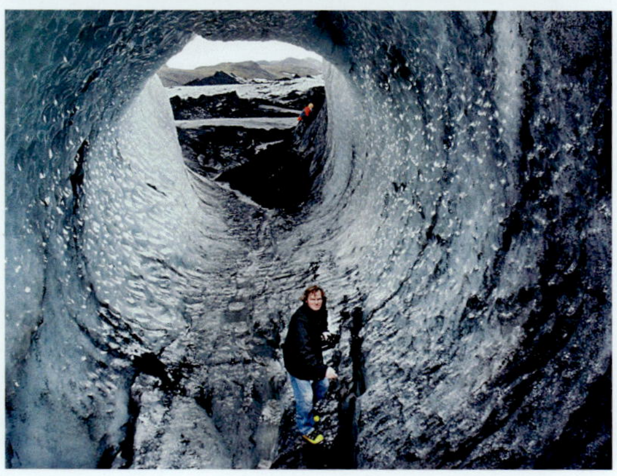

Being an Icelandic native was invaluable. There were many places that I was familiar with and I revisited them while scouting. Yet, there were also many locations that I still needed to find. Location scouting is time consuming and I spent a lot of hours on the road. Iceland is surrounded by a two-lane highway that circles most of the entire coastline of the island. The interior of Iceland is primarily a barren landscape of rock and glacier. Once you go off the main road onto the secondary roads in the countryside they become much smaller and are often unpaved.

There are vast areas in Iceland that are unbounded and unrestricted. There are few fences, signs, or anything else that limits your view. As long as you stay on the road, or a clearly defined path, the country is an open landscape. Prior to this project, I had traveled extensively in the country. This was a great aid in knowing what locations I wanted to work in, and how to get there. Oftentimes it was just a matter of finding the right formation by exploring the terrain that was off the beaten path.

Sometimes a friend or family member would accompany me while scouting. In the beginning, they enjoyed coming along and I would use them as a stand-in for the model. However, over time it became tedious for them due to the constant interruptions along the way as I pulled over to photograph potential locations. In the end, most of the scouting I did for locations became a solo venture.

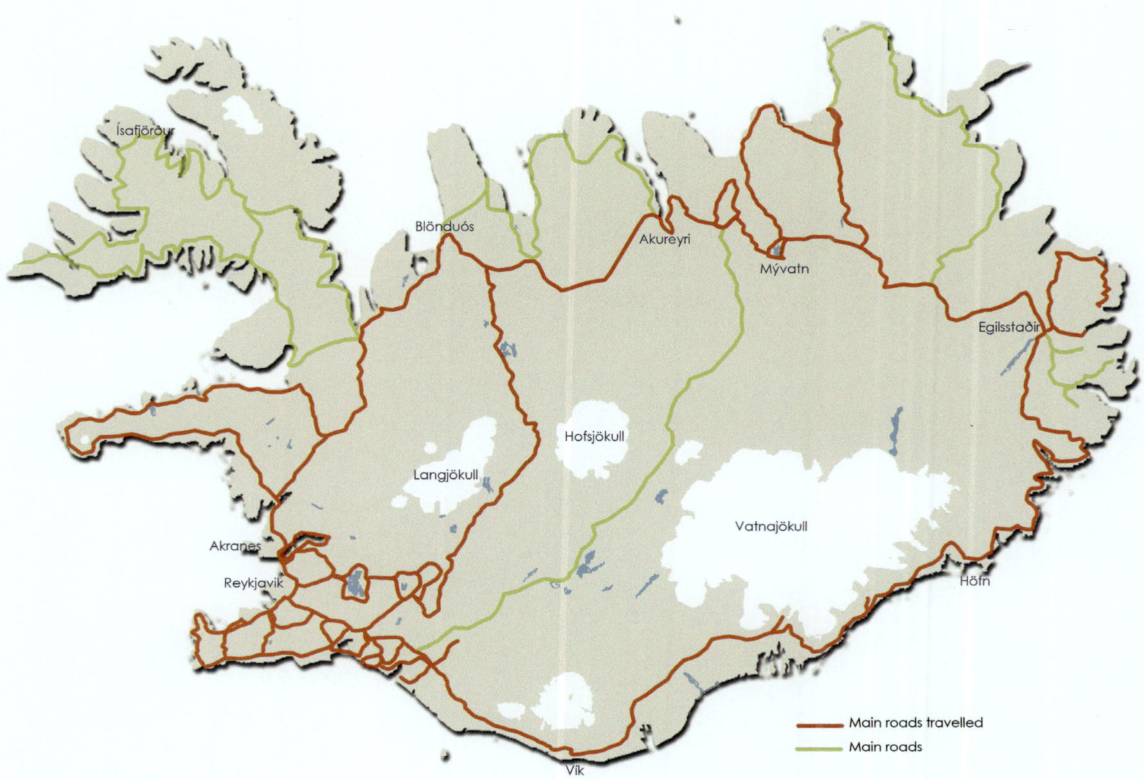

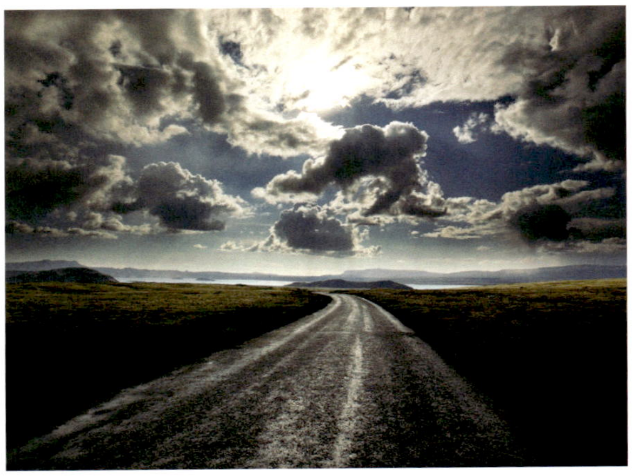

There is a saying in Iceland, "If you don't like the weather, wait 5 minutes." The weather can be very unpredictable and I had to keep a close eye on it. As long as it didn't rain heavily, I could photograph. This was true both for location scouting and while photographing the models. The day might start out with clear skies and we would take off for the location in good spirits, only to arrive in a downpour of rain. One particular summer the weather was especially erratic and I had to turn back from a shoot several times before I even got one shot.

The temperature in Iceland in the summer is around 60 - 65° Fahrenheit (15-20° Celsius). It is not particularly warm, but very mild and pleasant. The ocean temperature is much colder and posing the models in more chilled conditions was a definite concern.

But, when there's good weather, it's wonderful. This is especially evident in the light in Iceland. Being so far north, the sun is never directly overhead; it comes down from the side. It's a directional light and if there is a thin cloud cover then the sky becomes like a natural soft box. This creates a gorgeous light to photograph models in. That is one of the plusses of having that kind of weather. When the sun is out, almost anytime of day has great light. Because of its closeness to the Arctic Circle, Iceland has light nights in the summer time.

In the middle of June I was photographing until midnight. The sun was still visible just above the horizon.

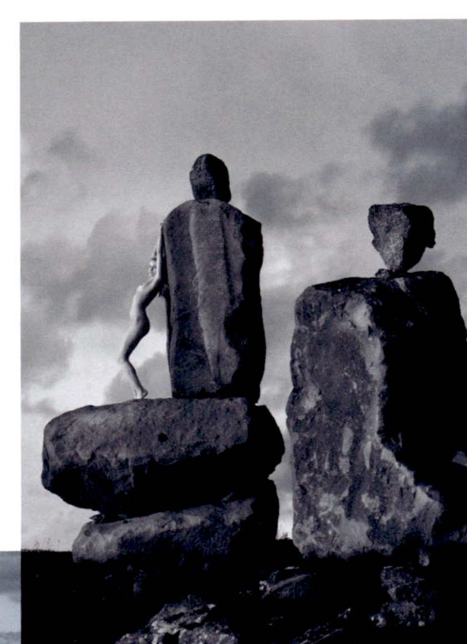

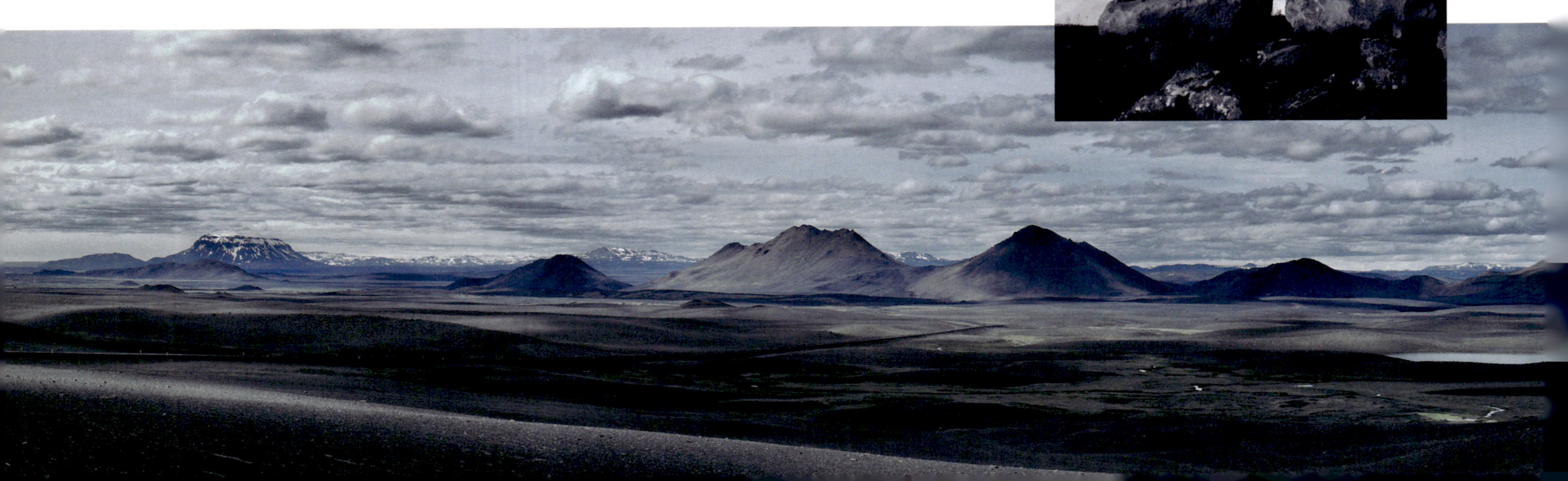

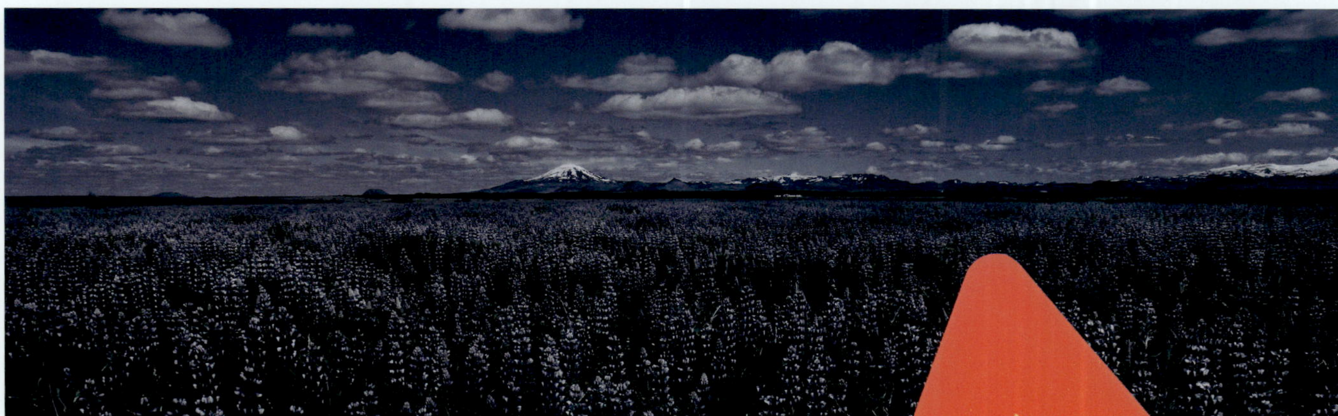

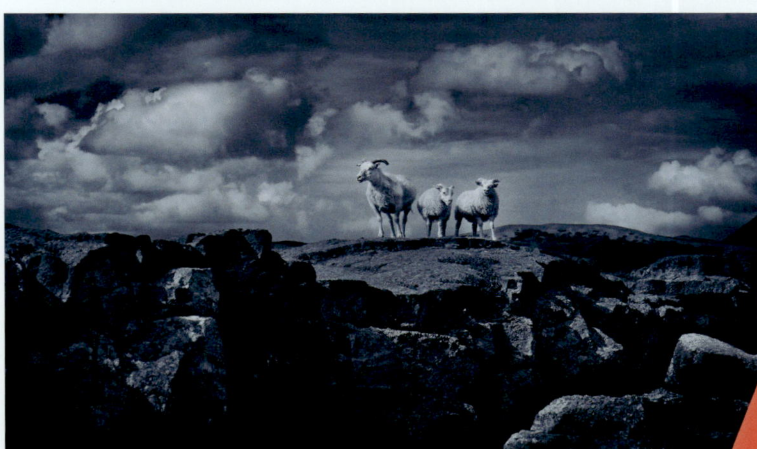

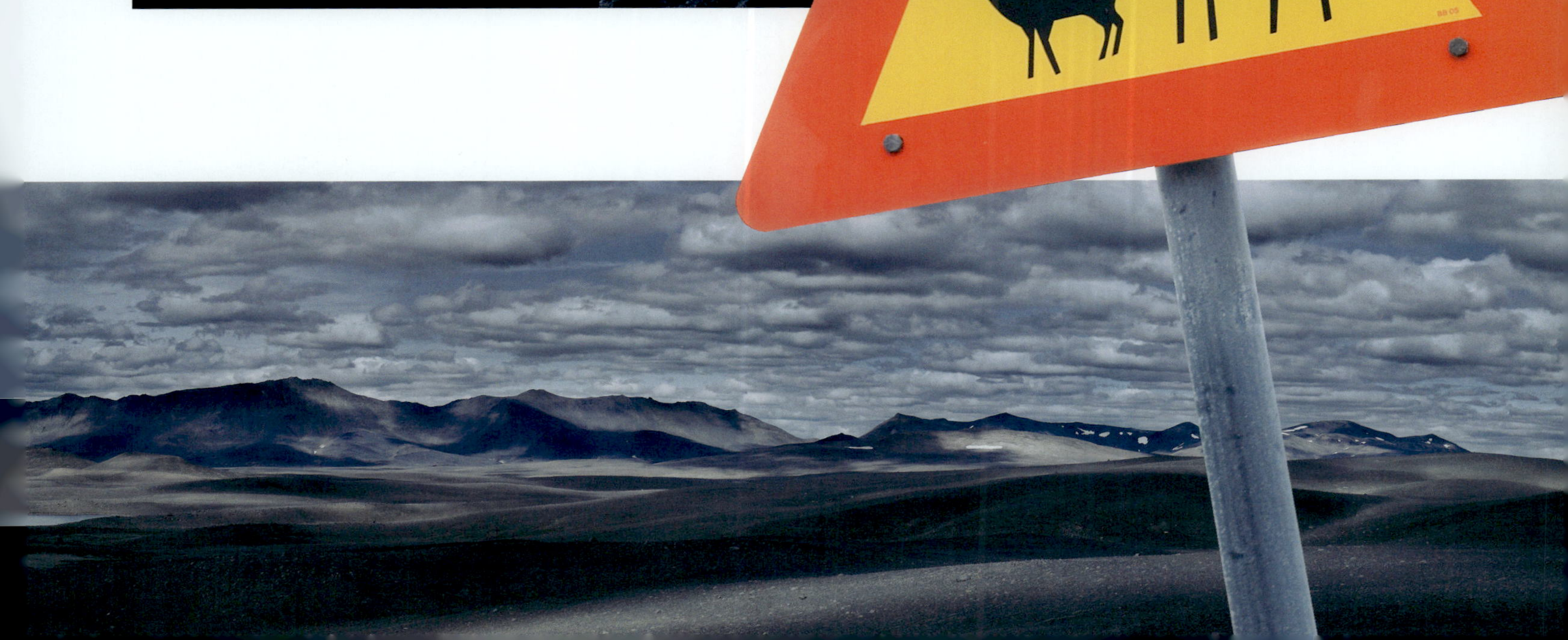

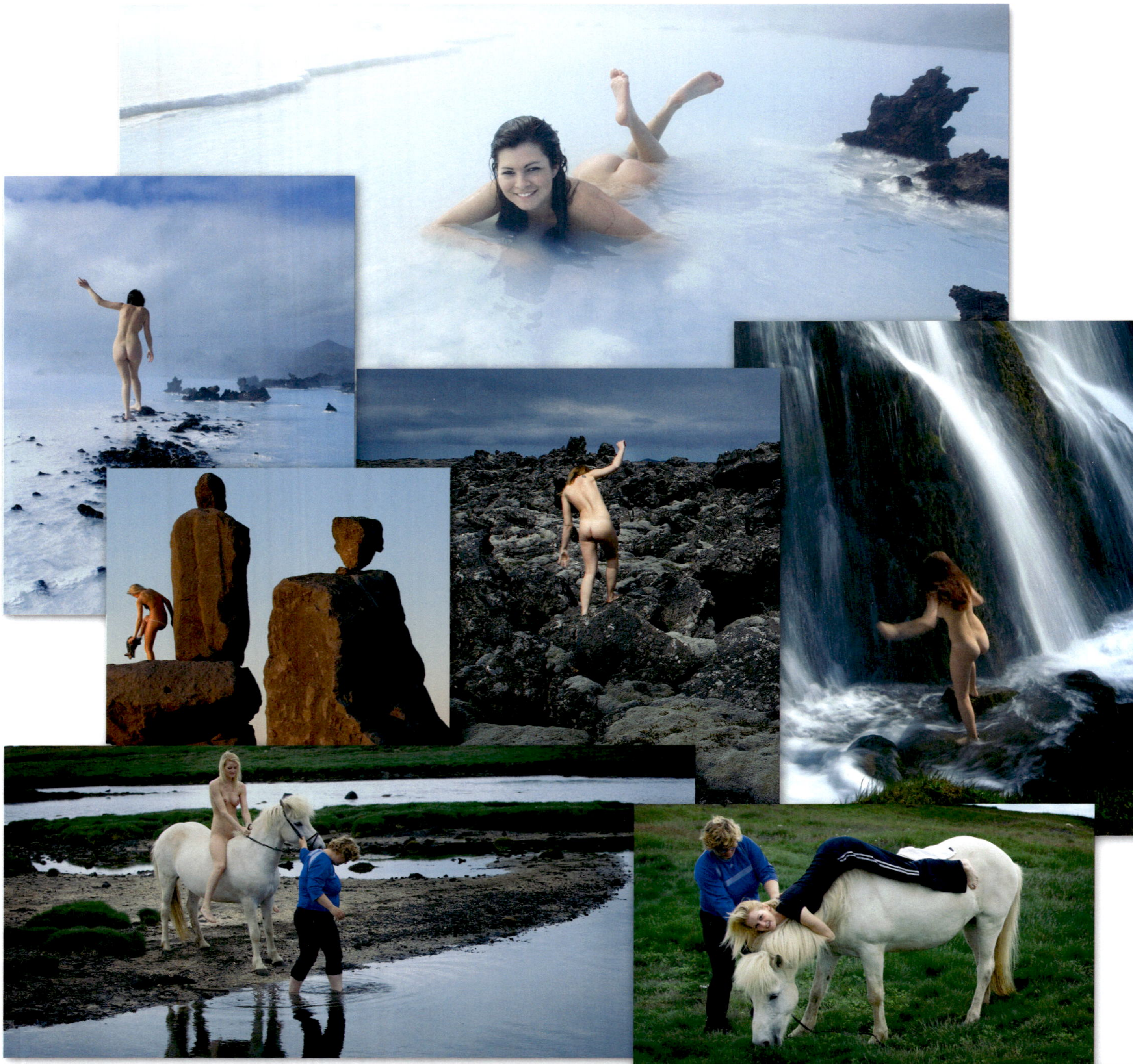

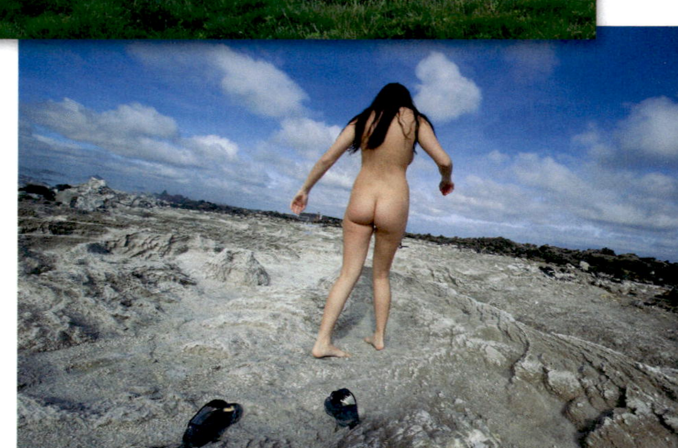

Although some of the women had modeled before, none of them were professionals and several had never modeled at all. They came from all walks of life – students, mothers, and business women. This was not always an easy assignment, given the climate and the terrain and some of the photos clearly belie this difficulty. I was very lucky in that the models believed in the project. This helped on the difficult days when we were both aiming for the most artistic shot possible in spite of the weather or rocky landscape.

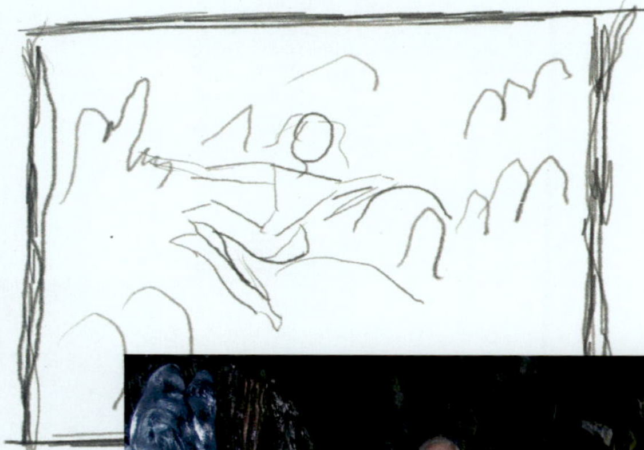

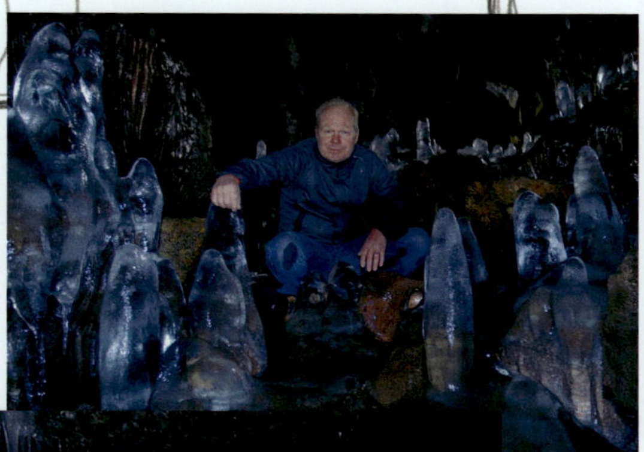

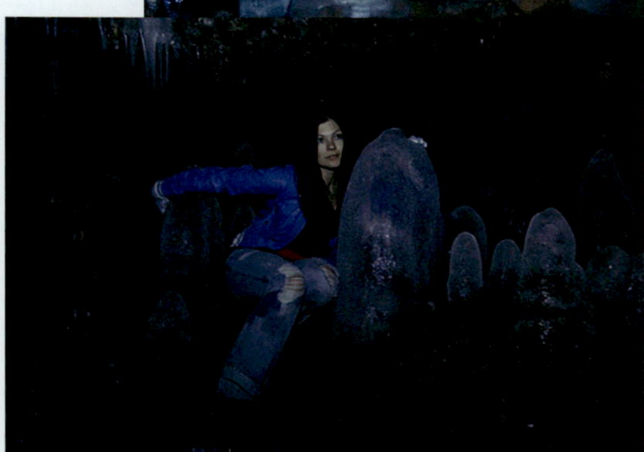

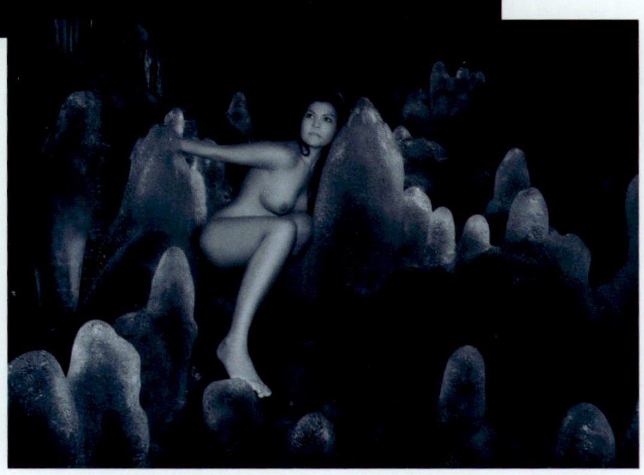

Preplanning the entire shoot was crucial. But, it is one thing to sketch out an idea and quite another to make it work in person. I could picture a location in my mind, but when I scouted it physically, I often had to re-think specific problems inherent to that landscape or the weather conditions there. Often the need for speed was essential in capturing the shot. This was especially true in circumstances where the model would be in an uncomfortable situation, like posing on sharp rock, craggy lava, ice, or in a popular public location. During those moments, it was always necessary to shoot within a short window of time.

One shoot day we were in a national park on a trail up off the main path. I had an assistant stationed with a walkie-talkie down below to alert us to when anyone was approaching. This gave us maybe 30 seconds to stop the shoot and have the model cover up.

On another occasion, we were shooting in an underground ice cave. The darkness, the slippery floor, and the frozen coldness of the ice all presented their own problems. On the day of the shoot, the model, an assistant and myself strapped spikes to our shoes and brought flashlights to reach the location. The strobes had to be hand held, since there was no place to set down the light stands. We practiced the poses with the model clothed first before shooting. In this instance, it shortened the time the model was in direct contact with the ice and enabled us to pull off the shot without her freezing.

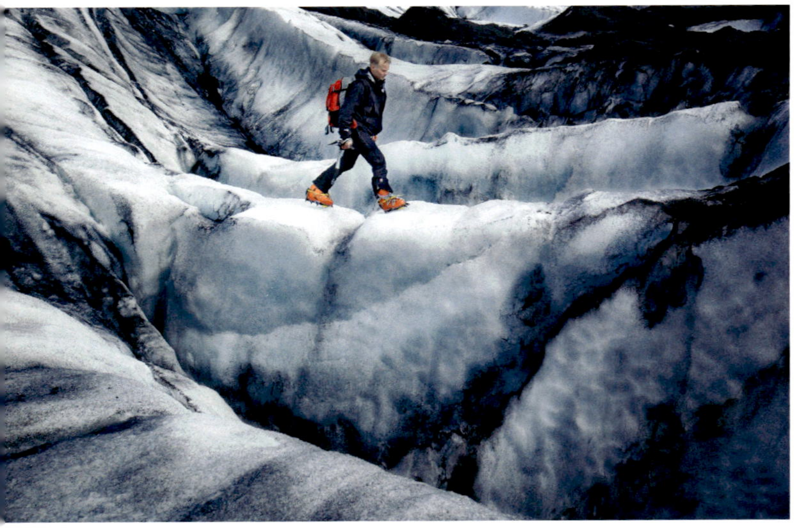

Most of the images were photographed in the summertime because of the light and temperate weather. However, there were a few locations that I wanted to photograph that could only be shot when it was cold enough to have ice, but also warm enough for the model. Timing my return to Iceland from Los Angeles specifically for these shots was critical. My friend Kristján who is both an experienced ice climber and photographer helped me plan the ideal time of year to return. We decided that early spring would be the best opportunity to capture the ice shots.

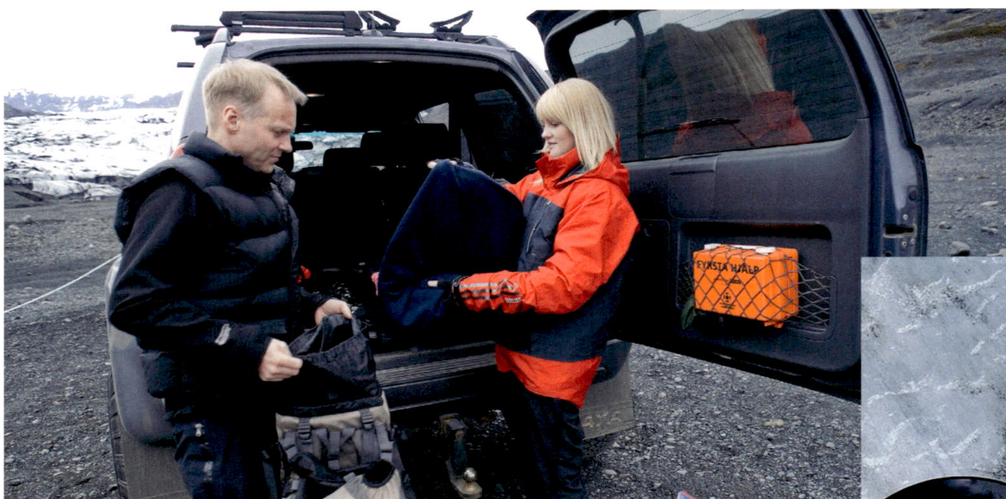

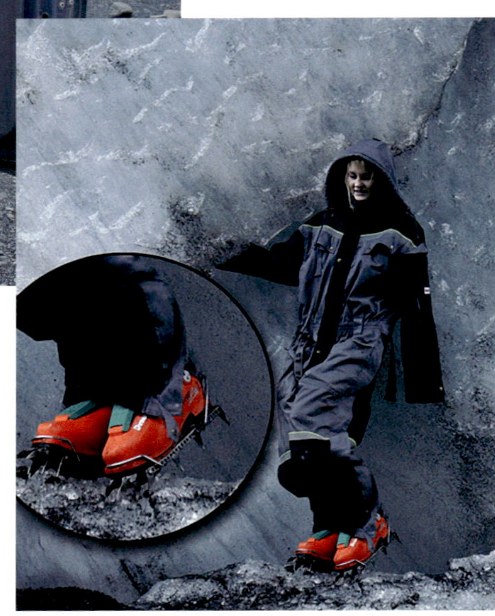

There are known ice caves in many of the glaciers that don't melt in the summertime. However, in the last few years these caves have been disappearing, and many are gone. My goal was to find a visual alternative, a wall of ice or a place where the melting ice carved out a giant hole or a cave. These are random formations and usually melt away later in the summer.

Kristján and I were well equipped with ice climbing gear when we set out to hike up one of the glaciers. Carrying the photo equipment proved quite heavy and the climb was difficult and exhausting over the slippery terrain. But, after a few hours we got lucky and came upon an ice cave that was perfect. I knew it was imperative to photograph it as soon as possible, before it began melting, which would force the roof to cave in.

We returned to the ice cave a few days later with the model, but none of us were really prepared for just how cold it was. Despite wearing sweaters, down jackets, caps and gloves, the cold still pierced through the layers. When it came time to shoot, we had maybe 2 to 3 minutes tops to get the shot off before the model had to be bundled in a blanket and removed from the ice. It then took 10-15 minutes to warm her back up before we could start another round of shooting. Because of the ice, the cold conditions, and the location, this was one of the more difficult photographs to create.

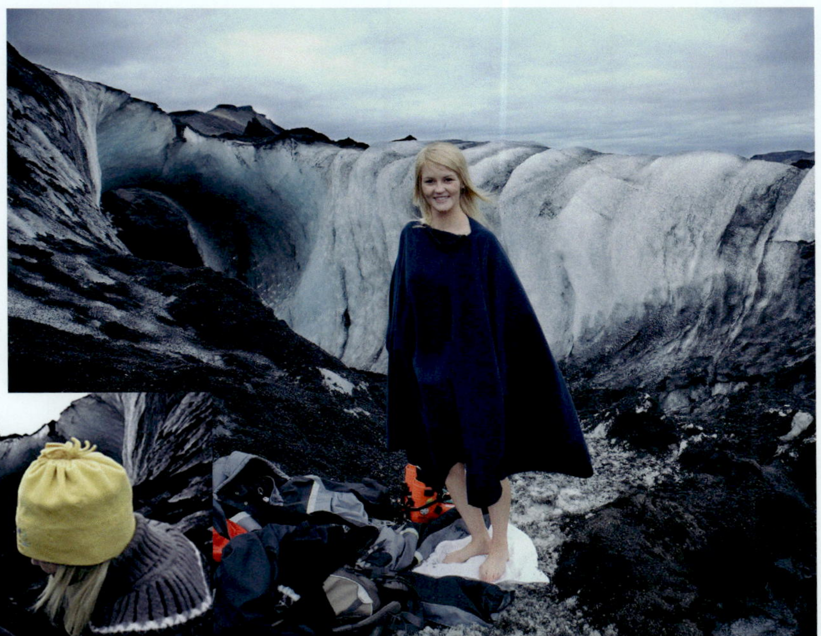

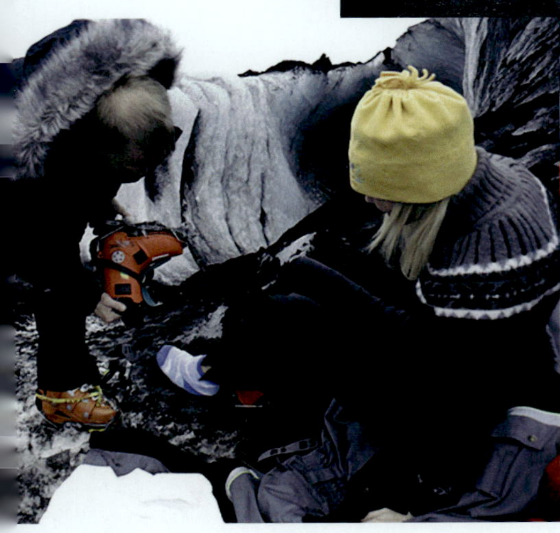

All projects come together by the sum of their parts and this project was no different. I feel privileged to have been able to photograph the wondrous landscapes in Iceland. I am also indebted to the graciousness of the models, who collaborated with me on this project. To everyone who assisted me...whether driving, setting lights or simply giving feedback, your help and input was invaluable and greatly appreciated.

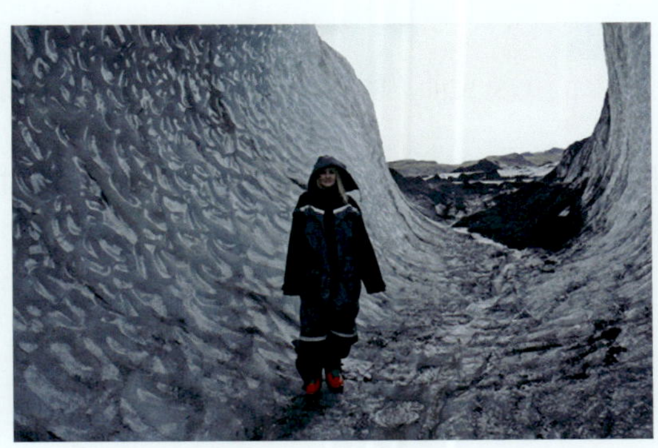

Sigthor Markusson

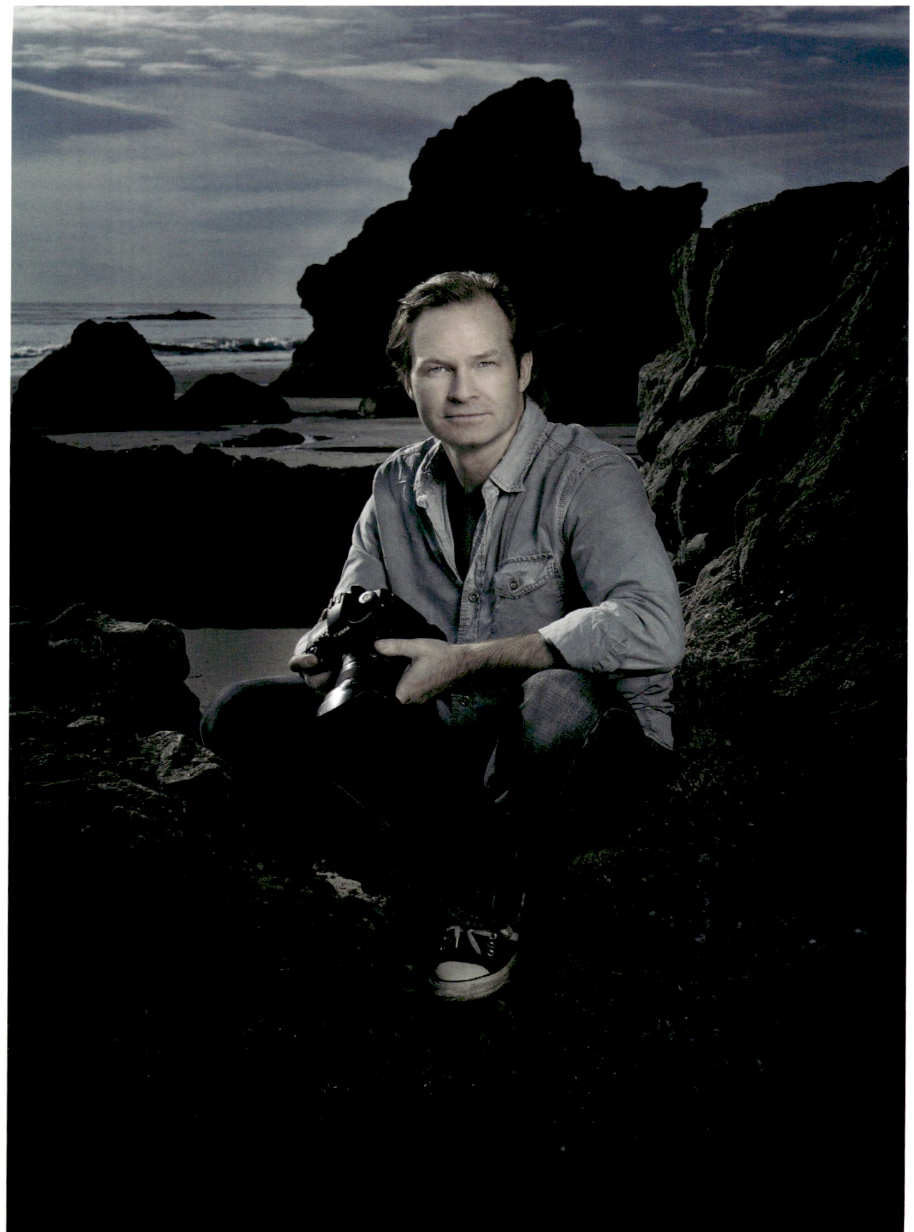

Sigthor Markusson

Sigthor Markusson was born in Iceland. He studied at Brooks Institute of Photography in Santa Barbara, California, graduating with honors. He currently is a professional photographer working in Los Angeles. This is his first book of photos.

Anna S. Björnsdóttir
Born 30th of November 1948 in Reykjavík/Iceland

Elementary School, Seminarium of Iceland from 1965 to 1969 and was working as a teacher from 1969 to 2008, when she retired. Anna also worked as a free-lance journalist in Iceland, from 1985-1992.
She became a member of Writers Union of Iceland in 1991 and her first book of poetry „Örugglega ég“ *Definitely me* was published in 1988, followed by 13 other books over the next 20 years. Two translated into English *By the Seaside* and *Currents* and two books translated into Danish „Mens solen stadig er fremme“ and „Virkelig mig“ which was published in Denmark in 2008, by Medan forlag, www.ullatarp.dk
Anna´s poetry has been included in many anthologies, both in Iceland and abroad and she is a recipient of various grants. The Reykjavik City Library´s Web site www.literature.is contains informations of her and samples of her work in English.

English translation by Hallberg Hallmundsson and Karl J. Guðmundsson

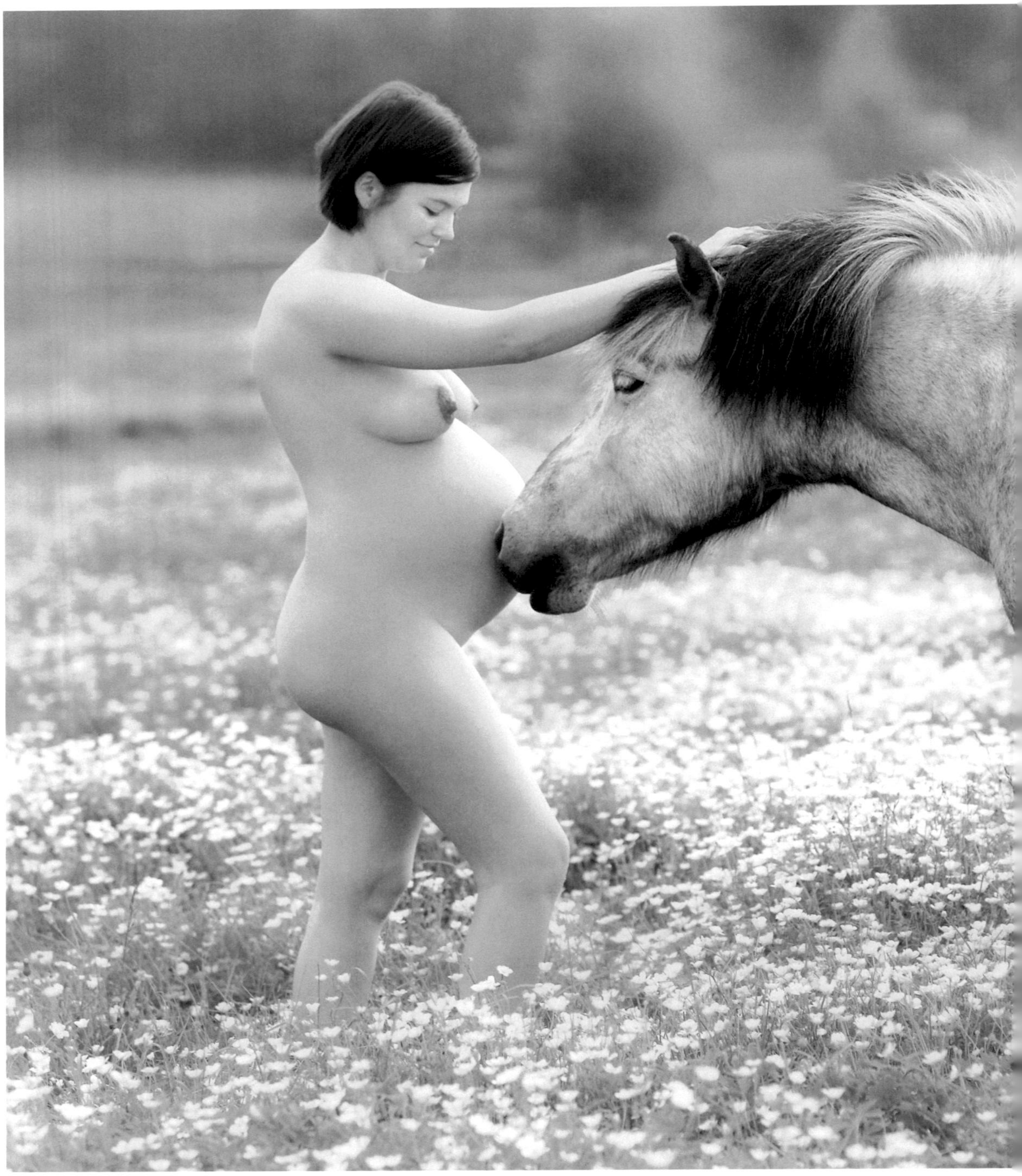

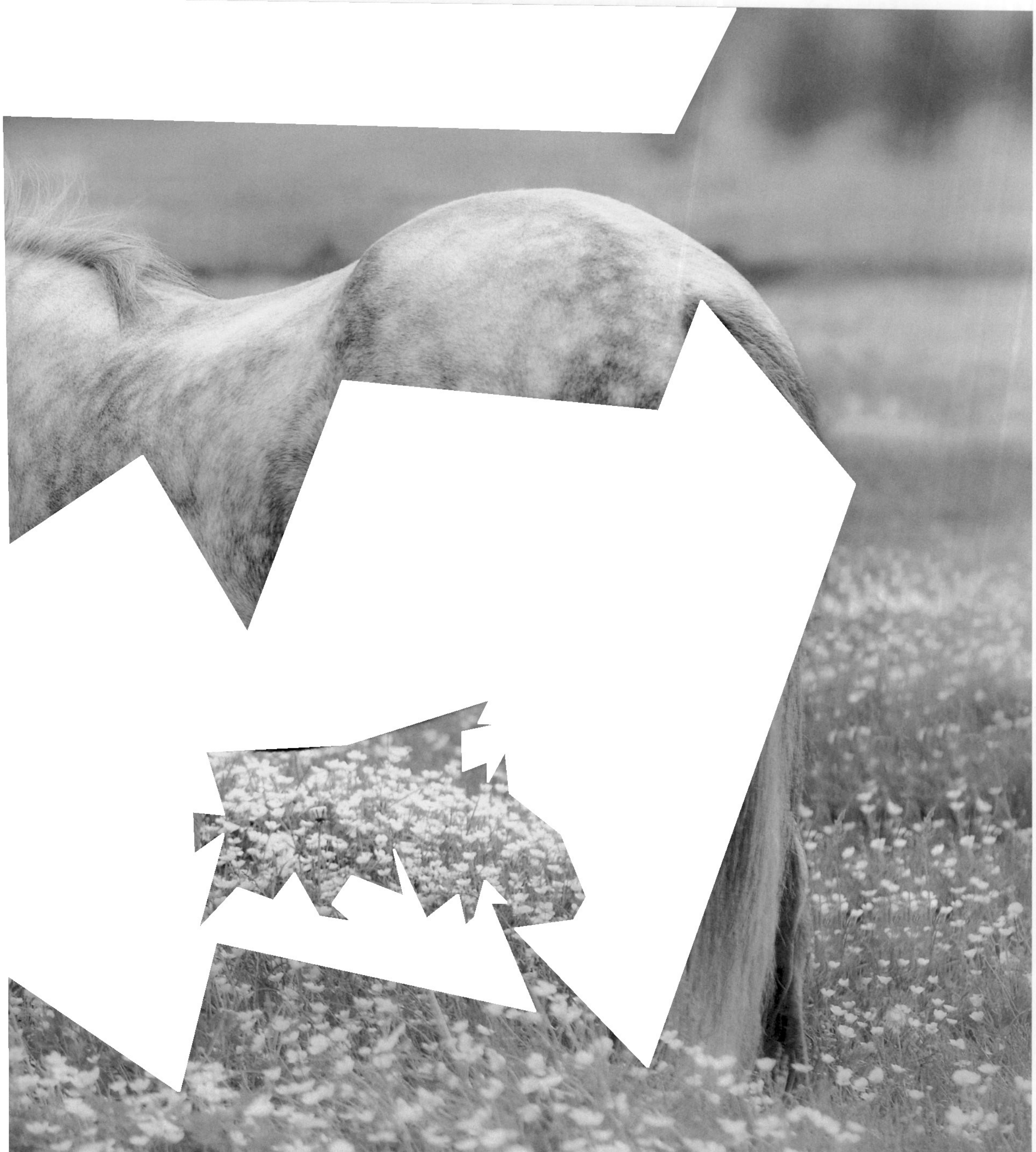